THE COMPANY WE KEEP

THE COMPANY WE KEEP

An Intimate Celebration of Opera Australia

TEXT BY ANNAROSA BERMAN   PHOTOGRAPHS BY BRIDGET ELLIOT

opera
australia

Currency Press, Sydney

First published in 2006 by
Opera Australia
PO Box 291,
Strawberry Hills NSW 2012 Australia
www.opera-australia.org.au

in association with Currency Press
PO Box 2287,
Strawberry Hills NSW 2012 Australia
www.currency.com.au
enquiries@currency.com.au

In accordance with the requirement of the Australian Media and
Arts Alliance, the publisher has made every effort to identify, and
gain permission of, the artists who appear in the photographs.

National Library of Australia Cataloguing-in-Publication Data:
Berman, Annarosa.
    The company we keep : an intimate celebration of Opera
    Australia.
    Includes index.
    ISBN 978 0 86819 786 9.
    ISBN 0 86819 786 6.
    1. Opera Australia - History. 2. Opera companies - Australia
    - History. 3. Opera - Production and direction - Australia. I.
    Elliot, Bridget. II. Opera Australia. III. Title.
    782.10994

Photograph on page ii: Mezzo-soprano Deborah Humble
    and baritone Han Lim in *Manon*.
Cover photographs by Bridget Elliot.
Cover Design by Linda Matthews, Opera Australia.
Typeset in Bliss 2 11/17
Printed by Fivestargrafx, Adelaide

CONTENTS

Right: Tools of the trade adorn a wall in Wardrobe.

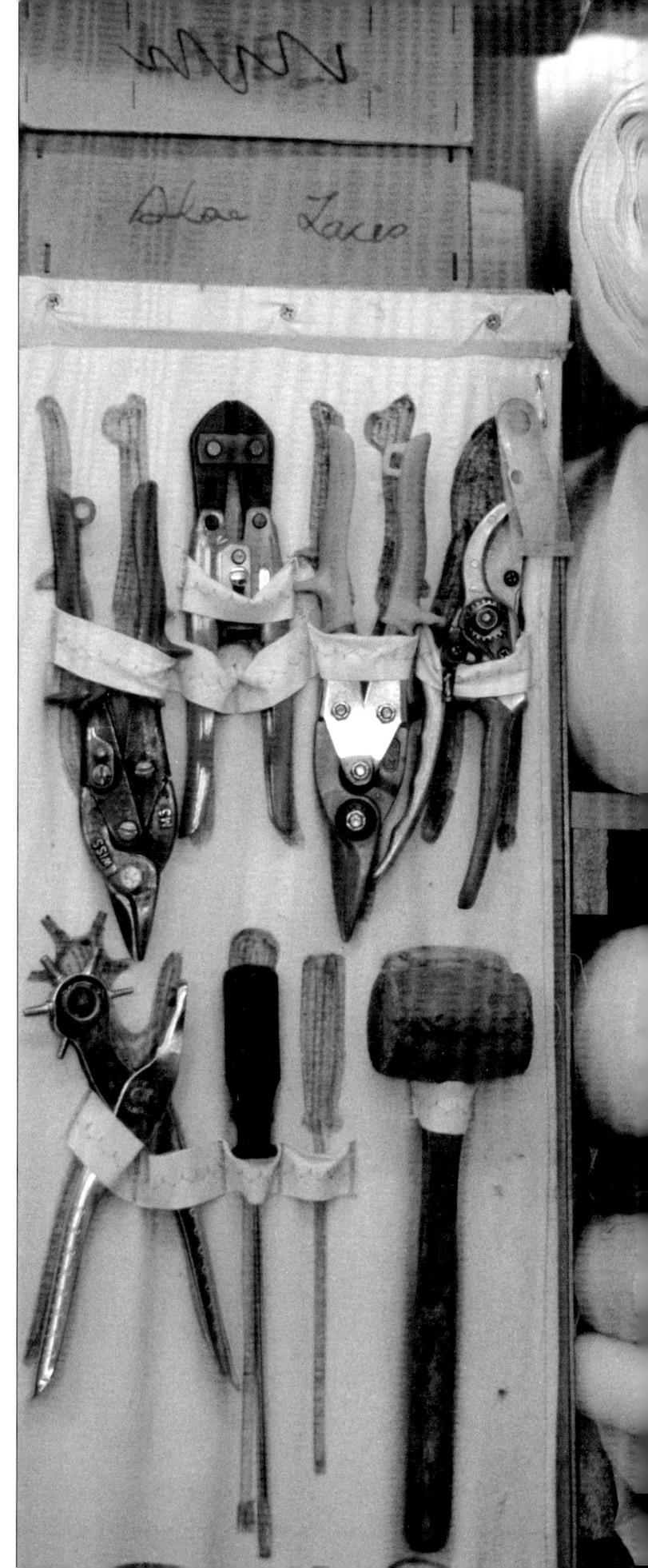

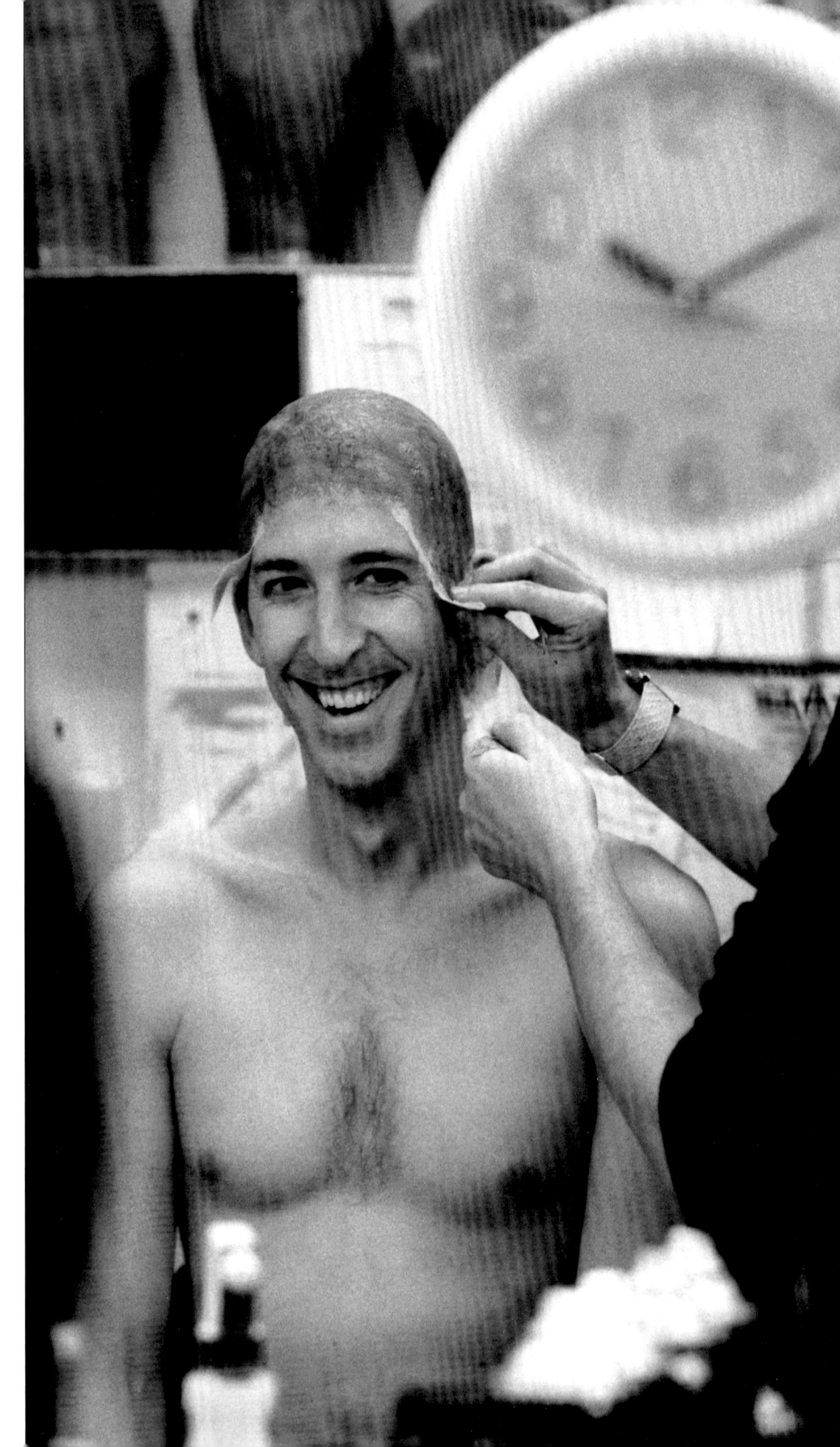

ACKNOWLEDGMENTS

The Company We Keep: an Intimate Celebration of Opera Australia is the result of an idea that was born in 2003. Regular visits to the Opera Centre to produce illustrated articles for various publications inspired us to want to tell what seemed to us to be the 'unsung' story of Opera Australia.

Every time we entered the Centre there was music coming from somewhere—even from the 'facilities', an otherwise untoward area of the building blessed with a resonant acoustic. Then we discovered Wardrobe, an airy workspace filled with swathes of fabric and seamstresses beavering over fabulous designs. In another corner of the building, Wigs, where staff thread human hair strand by strand and downstairs, Workshop, where even building an aeroplane is not too much of a challenge.

OA's fiftieth birthday presented an opportunity to tell the story of the people and processes behind the music and drama presented onstage almost every night of the year at either the Sydney Opera House or the Arts Centre.

While there are more people involved than we can mention here, we would like especially to thank marketing and communications director Liz Nield and chief executive Adrian Collette, for embracing this project; acting marketing director Judith James; publications manager Michael Pedersen for steering the process through to completion; national publicist Emma Williams for setting up many interviews; assistant publicist Milou de Castellane; senior stage manager Bianca Esther; the 2005 **Oz**Opera crew; design manager Linda Matthews for the cover; and all the people at OA who have welcomed us into their midst. We are honoured that Dame Joan Sutherland has contributed her good wishes.

We thank Victoria Chance, Kate Florance and Claire Grady of Currency Press and John Budgen of BudgeInk, for turning our words and pictures into this beautiful book.

Among friends and colleagues thanks go to Ian Gunn, for the title; Shelley Kenigsberg; Ian Lever; Claude Ho; Michael Frankel and Susie Lorentz. Last but not least, our love and thanks go to our husbands, Charles Berman and David Goldberg, for their support during life with the book.

Annarosa Berman and Bridget Elliot,
Sydney, April 2006.

Left: The clock ticks for tenor Kanen Breen as he prepares for the dress rehearsal of *Dido and Aeneas*.

PRELUDE

This book is timely and important not merely because it presents a record of Australia's national company on its fiftieth birthday, but also because it reflects the miracle that is opera and the odds over which Opera Australia has triumphed to celebrate its fiftieth year.

I wish the company well on this very special occasion. As the passion and dedication conveyed in *The Company We Keep* demonstrates, I am sure it will continue to present great opera long into the future.

Dame Joan Sutherland OM, AC, DBE
Switzerland, April 2006

Joan Sutherland

Left: Soprano Miriam Gordon-Stewart looks for her cue to enter the stage in Act III of *Fledermaus*.

CHAPTER ONE

FIT AT FIFTY

It's an amazing story, how a tenacious band of artists that started with a season of Mozart operas in 1956 flourished into a thriving powerhouse; a full-time ensemble company of international repute…

The words—characteristically enthusiastic—are those of Opera Australia music director Richard Hickox; the 'band of artists' the people—butchers, newsagents and pharmacists among them—who half a century ago gave up their day jobs to embark on a season of *Don Giovanni, The Magic Flute, The Marriage of Figaro* and *Così fan tutte* to celebrate the Mozart bicentenary.

At the launch of Opera Australia's 2006 Sydney season, Hickox told a story that suggests one reason why this part-time troupe of singers, instrumentalists and theatre types burgeoned into one of Australia's flagship arts companies. Not long after the British conductor had agreed to make Sydney his home, the top job at English National Opera became available. A British journalist interviewing him at the Sydney Opera House at the time asked if he felt frustrated at having effectively disqualified himself from the ENO position. Hickox recalled that it was a magnificent summer's day and that through the window they could see brightly coloured sails bobbing on the waves while a cluster of ferries passed underneath the Sydney Harbour Bridge. He remembered looking at the ferries and the sails, then turning to the reporter. 'Are you *mad*?' he asked.

It's an attitude that permeates OA, from its top music and administrative personnel to the seamstresses, wigmakers, drivers and technicians who cement the company together. Staff in Sydney and Melbourne consider themselves lucky to be able to earn a living doing what they love to do. Chief executive Adrian Collette does not exaggerate when he says: 'Morale is not an issue here. If you want to work in opera in Australia, the national company is the place to be.'

Left: Taking stock: Bass Conal Coad in costume for *Manon*.

To Collette, being 'national' means offering a countrywide resource for opera as well as sharing technical and manufacturing expertise with the State companies—when the State Opera of South Australia did its *Ring* cycle in Adelaide in 2004, for example, OA sent over its head of music, its senior stage manager and a production manager 'because in Australia no one else really knows how to run repertory opera'.

'National' also means regional performances through OA's touring arm, **Oz**Opera, and mainstage productions in two capital cities. Once a baritone with the Victoria State Opera (VSO), Collette believes it's good for the company to have a presence in two cities. 'We have a fifty-year history in Melbourne and we look forward to a continued commitment there.'

Richard Hickox makes his debut as OA's music director with *The Love for Three Oranges*.

Icons and milestones

The name Opera Australia dates from 1996, when The Australian Opera merged with the VSO, a step that was not universally applauded. Nonetheless, there have been many highlights in the company's fifty-year history. Moffatt Oxenbould, artistic director for fifteen years until 1999, stresses that the true milestones are the excellent performances the company has given in the past five decades.

But he singles out a few other highlights for mention. The defining one was the 1956 Mozart bicentenary, which harnessed the talent of the time. Next, the company's participation in the 1965 season presented by Joan Sutherland, Richard Bonynge and theatrical entrepreneur J. C. Williamson enticed many to join Australia's growing community of opera enthusiasts. An OA forerunner, the Elizabethan Theatre Trust Opera Company, provided the chorus and stage management for the season.

At the time and throughout the 1960s the building on Bennelong Point was taking shape, says Oxenbould, and 'people were asking, "Is it a tortoise? Is it a nun?"'. In 1967 the New South Wales State Government provided a grant towards the formation of a permanent company for the Opera House and in the same year the company introduced subscriptions. Both were milestones in the history of Australian opera.

The greatest turning point of all, though, was the opening of the Sydney Opera House in 1973. The beauty of the building exceeded the wildest expectations of those who had been awaiting its completion, but its interior was not everything they had hoped for. 'We'd been dreaming about walking through the pearly gates into Paradise', Oxenbould recalls. Instead, tucked away under the Opera Theatre stage they found the pit, a cramped space with a tinny acoustic. Despite the building's limitations, Australia remains the only country in the world with an opera house for an icon.

In 1974 Sutherland returned to do *The Tales of Hoffmann,* a landmark production which provided the company operating under the white sails with a 'Good Housekeeping' seal—if it was good enough for Joan Sutherland it was good enough for Australia. Eleven years later The Australian Opera moved to the Opera Centre in Surry Hills, which united its rehearsal, administrative and manufacturing operations under one roof.

Almost a decade lapsed before Oxenbould's Next Big Thing: the success of Baz Luhrmann's *A Midsummer Night's Dream* at the 1994 Edinburgh Festival. The production, which presented Scottish audiences with a distinctly Australian version of a British opera, marked a turning point in local production history which until then—with the exception of Neil Armfield's *The Cunning Little Vixen*— had emulated European trends.

Executive producer Stuart Maunder directs members of the chorus in a rehearsal of *Romeo and Juliet.*

In 1999, the year in which Oxenbould announced his retirement as artistic director, Simone Young was appointed music director–designate, marking the final highlight of his tenure with OA. Young was the company's first music director since Richard Bonynge left The Australian Opera in 1986. Her term remains a creative milestone in company history, even though she returned to Europe after differences about repertoire choice—OA could not afford to put on the operas the conductor was keen to present—led to a difficult and controversial decision not to extend her contract.

Tout ensemble

For Richard Hickox, her successor, OA's attraction lies in its being 'one of the world's last great ensemble companies'. Many illustrious houses have permanent choruses and orchestras, but few still employ full-time singers. European and American companies tend to cut costs by flying in principals and using singers from young artist programs in minor roles. At OA however, where engaging an overseas singer involves a trek across continents, maintaining an ensemble remains essential.

The soloists on OA's payroll—around twenty of them—create an agreeable working environment for conductors and directors. 'Conductors enjoy the opportunity to mould a team', Hickox says. The regular addition of international guest artists like Philip Langridge, or of Australians with international careers—Cheryl Barker, Peter Coleman-Wright, Yvonne Kenny—ensures a 'potent' artistic mix.

American director Francesca Zambello, who directed the company's acclaimed productions of *Lady Macbeth of Mtsensk* (2002) and *The Love for Three Oranges* (2005), enjoys the sense of camaraderie and ease that comes from working with an ensemble: 'When you direct people who have been working together for years, you cut to the chase much quicker', she says. She also values the insight into a singer's range provided by knowing the other roles in the company repertoire he or she has sung.

In some respects ensemble companies can set their own standards. European opera houses, because of their geographic proximity to each other, can fly in singers at short notice, but the practice does not always lead to first-rate performances. As Moffatt Oxenbould observes: 'The greatness of opera lies in its uniting extraordinary forces—music, drama and art—and if you unite them well you have something that has triple the power.' But if there's nothing better than a good opera performance, there's nothing worse than a bad one: 'A singer who arrives on Sunday, starts rehearsing on Monday and is still trying to memorise the piece by Thursday, drags down the entire production.'

Above: Former artistic director Moffatt Oxenbould congratulates soprano Elena Prokina after opening night of the 2006 revival of his production of *Madama Butterfly*.

Right: Former OA music director Simone Young rehearses the AOBO.

There are, of course, disadvantages to performing regularly with the same colleagues. One of them is that it can be difficult to maintain a fresh approach. 'It's all too easy to say, "'It's *Tosca* again darlings!"', Oxenbould points out. And, as former Australian Opera music director Richard Bonynge remarks, an ensemble company is to some extent restricted to selecting repertoire for which it has the voices.

To the people whose careers are sustained by OA, the advantages of being part of the ensemble outweigh such drawbacks. As Collette says: 'Occasionally musicians and administrative staff get tired and grumpy because they're overworked, but no one forgets what we're here to do, which is to get the curtain up.'

In doing so—well over 200 times a year—OA builds its future. No one pretends that it will ever be able to compete for star-studded casts, but, says Collette, in fostering its ensemble to the point where its artists are on the world's stages, as a company it becomes internationally relevant. 'That has to be the journey for the next fifty years. It's nothing that's not happening already, but we have to continue to provide our artists with an environment in which they can thrive.'

OA provides such an environment to its managers, designers and directors too, and like its singers, they build bridges to the international opera world.

But everybody who works for the company helps to get the curtain up. Artistic leaders conceive of seasons that balance visions with budgets; directors and designers dream up gripping ways of presenting those operas; technical staff turn concepts into sets, props and costumes; conductors, orchestral musicians and choristers transform dots on pages into music.

At the final dress rehearsal, backstage staff provide the support that enables the many creative visions to merge into the extraordinary fusion of music, drama and art that is opera.

Left: Conductor Richard Bonynge studies the score before a piano dress rehearsal of *Romeo and Juliet*.

Above: Chief executive Adrian Collette and chairman of the Board, Gordon Fell, in the Sydney Opera Centre boardroom.

CHAPTER TWO

A SEASON IS BORN

Emma Murphy, OA finance director from 1998 until 2005, tells the story about the new Board member who came to meet senior management at the Opera Centre. Managers and directors were sitting around the boardroom table talking shop and drinking tea when he asked: 'So what happens if you miss your box office target?' 'We have a deficit', someone informed him.

He was horrified.

'But that—unfortunately—is what has to happen', Murphy says, with the patience of a pre-school teacher explaining gravity to a five-year-old.

Risky business

Public subsidy provides 30% of OA's income; fundraising and contributions 15%. The latter, says marketing and communications director Liz Nield, has remained flat in recent years, so that the real pressure is on the remaining source of revenue: the box office, at once the company's main source of income and its biggest risk. 'We live or die by it', says chief executive Adrian Collette, 'so if you want to know what I think about, I think about how ticket sales are doing. It has greater capacity to derail this company than anything else and our planning for it has to be acute'.

Although it cuts where it can, OA's survival depends on growing income rather than curbing costs because the lion's share of its expenses are incurred through labour. Opera companies have limited opportunities for reducing the size of their workforces: Verdi wrote *La traviata* for an orchestra of about 67 and a chorus of about 66, and although a 21st-century company wishing to stage the work can trim at the edges, it still needs more or less that number of artists. (Orchestra members joke that increasing tempos can save as much as ten minutes a night.)

Left: Attention to detail: one of designer Roger Kirk's costume sketches for *Manon*.

Collette looks on the bright side. 'Budgetary restrictions keep us in touch with our audience—we never do things just for the sake of it', he says. He is grateful for existing grants and does not foresee—or expect—that OA will ever receive the level of public funding (around 80%) that many European houses get. But a little bit more would go a

long way. 'In a company with a $55-million turnover, even $50,000 can make a big impact on decisions about repertoire, artists and the scale of the program', he says. And he feels strongly that OA's Melbourne operation, which functions outside the turbo-charged tourism environment that fills the Sydney Opera House, needs at least 45% in public subsidy if it is to offer patrons a program as varied as the one Sydney audiences enjoy.

Always bearing in mind the demands of the box office, Collette's planning for a new season starts with some overriding consideration—not necessarily economic— which varies from year to year. In 2004, for example, after OA had experienced an operating deficit in 2002, his instruction to staff was to get the company back in the black. While productions for which guest artists have already been contracted do not allow much room for manoeuvring, some shows are planned as little as eighteen months before opening night.

The 2004 artistic program was thus engineered to include *Baroque Masterworks*, an ingenious but relatively inexpensive double bill, as well as a commercial run of *The Mikado* in Melbourne. In 1999, another crisis year, the company went the other way, doing mega-popular productions for which it attracted record crowds. Such measures of crisis management, however, if repeated too often could cause a backlash. In any case the overriding concern for a year is often positive: scheduling for 2006, for example, was informed by a wish to celebrate the company's fiftieth birthday, which resulted in a program of works 'that have captured the imagination and won our hearts'.

What's on and who's who

Within the parameters of box office demands and the main theme for a particular year, OA's artistic leadership—Collette, executive producer Stuart Maunder and music director Richard Hickox—sets out to represent the four periods of opera (baroque or renaissance; classical; romantic; 20th century or contemporary) and to include works from the Italian, German, French, English and Slavic traditions. When selecting remounts, each production's history with the company is considered: *La traviata*, *La bohème* and *Carmen* can be staged more or less every third year; *Julius Caesar* every six or seven; *L'elisir d'amore* every five and *Lulu* every eight years. No opera company can afford to repeat the 'top ten' too often though because, as Maunder says, audiences will get sick of them.

OA stages at least four new productions each year. Hickox tries to include one 'novelty' or company debut—he's had great success with *Billy Budd* (1999), *Lady Macbeth of Mtsensk* (2002) and *The Love for Three Oranges* (2005)—along with replacements for two or three existing productions. (At any given time, the company has about ninety productions in its repertoire.)

OA calls these buildings home: the Arts Centre, Melbourne (left) and the Sydney Opera House (above).

Overleaf: On a smaller scale: designer Adam Gardnir's model for *The Beggar's Opera* (p.12); Costume detail from *Manon* (p.13).

Against the backdrop of these broad considerations, the reasons for including works vary widely. Maunder, for example, may advocate an opera that a particular director would like to do, while Hickox might support the inclusion of a work for which the perfect cast has presented itself.

Nowhere does the ensemble nature of the company come into play more obviously than in the casting process. 'If I were running Covent Garden', Hickox says, 'I would meet every director and conductor and we'd make a wish list for a cast and then we'd go and get it'. Retaining about twenty singers on contracts, on the other hand, is a complex operation: Hickox starts by putting down his ideal cast for every opera—a mixture of ensemble members and guest artists. He then checks that each singer has enough work to justify their contract.

Stephen Mould, senior repetiteur with OA before becoming its head of music in 2004, has the day-to-day knowledge of individual voices that Hickox, Collette and Maunder require to make their casting decisions. Mould, who studied at the Sydney Conservatorium and gained extensive experience as a repetiteur and conductor in Germany and England

before joining OA, says one of the most difficult aspects is choosing singers for roles they will only perform in two or three years' time. Booking artists early secures availability, at contemporary rates, but anything can happen in the interim—young singers may develop in unexpected ways, older singers may go downhill and stars may suffer vocal crises. 'Casting is not an exact science; you have to take some chances although hopefully not too many.'

Mould enjoys watching Collette, Hickox and Maunder come up with casts for the operas they've selected. 'On and off Stuart has been with the company for over twenty years, so he knows what all these people can do; Adrian has seen hundreds of performances and was a singer himself, so he brings that perspective to his decisions, but he also has an eye on who brings in dollars; Richard has a fundamentally musical approach and is guided by his ear—what it likes, what it accepts, what it doesn't accept.'

Crunching the numbers

Once casting has been done, an outline for the season's proposed repertoire and artists is handed to artistic administrator Ian McCahon, who puts together a preliminary schedule and advises on its achievability. In his office at the Opera Centre, McCahon, a music graduate who spent seven years in the chorus before moving into administration in 1993, calls up lists and graphs to illustrate his point. When he first tried to join management he was turned down because he lacked computer skills: 'They asked if I was computer literate and I had to admit I'd never switched on a PC in my life', he smiles. He bought a second-hand Apple Mac, spent six months studying the manual and applied again. That first computer and the time spent mastering it proved to be one of the best investments of his life.

He bases his cost estimate of the season's chosen repertoire on the way it's been cast ('Does the production require a soloist from outside the company or can it be cast from the ensemble?') and the other human resources it will need.

Technical administration director Chris Yates provides McCahon with cost estimates for sets, props and costumes. Yates, who started his career as an electrician for a Port Augusta power company ('Opera was not really prevalent there') before completing a technical production course in Adelaide, joined OA in 1990 as a lighting technician. (His father thought he was giving up a good job at the power company—he still thinks so.) Opera has kept Yates on board. 'It gets in your blood', he says. 'I love it.'

Sets and costumes comprise the bulk of technical expenses. It is easy for a piece like *Turandot* with its 120-strong cast to blow the budget, since each soloist, chorister, dancer and actor will need at least one costume. Even in a medium-sized production the costume budget can exceed $300,000. A new production of a decent-sized opera will require around $650,000 in technical production expenses.

Furthermore, a technically large piece with several complex sets that require a large crew for changeovers may compromise the company's ability to stage an evening performance of a different opera after a matinée. Length has to be considered too: an afternoon performance of the four-and-a-half-hour-long *Der Rosenkavalier* does not leave much time to install the set for the evening's show.

Reality check

Once technical and administrative calculations have been finalised, the draft for the new season is handed to marketing director Liz Nield, an Arts–Law graduate who worked as development manager for the Bell Shakespeare Company before joining OA in the late 1980s. She has the unenviable task of estimating the box office income that the operas on the list are likely to attract.

One of the many hand-made wigs from *Manon*.

Her forecasts are based on past experience and go a long way towards keeping OA out of the red, but they sometimes demand the sacrifice of cherished ideals. To celebrate the company's fiftieth birthday, for example, management had set its heart on remounting the colourful *Boris Godunov,* last done in 1986 and extremely well suited to the ensemble. 'It stayed in there while other shows went by the by', Nield recalls, 'but in the end taking it out boosted the budget by a couple of million dollars'. The opera combines a large cast with relatively small box office capacity. By comparison *Turandot*, which made it into the 2006 season, is also expensive to stage but redeems itself by selling 90–95% of its seats although its scale will still devour the bulk of its profit. If OA wanted to play it safe, it would substitute *Turandot* with *Così fan tutte,* which thanks to its small cast and orchestra needs to sell only 60% of its seats to recuperate costs, leaving a much greater margin for profit.

When a production is brought back for a second and third time, it usually needs an impetus, like a star in a leading role, to attract subscribers who have already seen it. On the other hand, an outstanding show will sometimes be brought back even if didn't sell well. *Batavia,* for example, was revived in Sydney in 2006 after its earlier Melbourne incarnation had played to 50% capacity audiences. *Lady Macbeth of Mtsensk,* though it lost money at the box office, was so highly regarded that it will be revived in due course. 'We bring back important pieces but we're realistic about what they're likely to earn', Nield says.

Forecasting is tricky, however: a production may be very successful the first time it is staged, create an even bigger buzz the second time around, then die at a third revival. 'The success of a show partly depends on the mood of an era', Nield says, or on the performance of a star performer, who may fail to inspire the audience. Luckily the opposite also happens: Nield recalls her anxiety about OA's 2001 production of *The Gypsy Princess*, 'but [tenor] Angus Wood was just so charming, and it sold and sold and sold'.

Dillon MacEwan constructs a prop in Workshop for *The Love for Three Oranges*.

When Nield has finalised her projections, they are handed to the finance director who, when the repertoire has been selected, the schedules checked, costs estimated and budgets predicted, goes through it all with a calculator and reports back on what Stuart Maunder calls 'the rude figures'.

Signing powers

Emma Murphy, a chartered accountant who joined OA in 1998 ('Before I came here I worked—Adrian dared me to say this—I worked in pest control, and I still do'), starts with the vision the artistic leadership is trying to achieve. 'They'll say they'd like to go off and do *Boris Godunov, Tannhäuser* and *The Ring'*, she explains, 'and you'd go well, that's great, we'll cost it, but it's not going to work'. She's been with OA long enough to predict what most productions will cost versus how much they will earn, and she can tell you instantly that choosing *The Barber of Seville* over *Sweeney Todd* will boost the budget by $200,000.

Opera is a risky business, Murphy says. 'Once the season is rolling, if a production doesn't fare as well as we'd hoped at the box office, there's not much we can do to recuperate our losses—we've contracted our artists and sold our subscriptions; we've started incurring costs and we can't suddenly trim them back by axing an act from *Tosca* or playing *Billy Budd* with half the required strings. That's why planning is so crucial for an opera company.'

Invariably, Murphy and her team discover that the artistic vision will cost $7 million more than the company can afford to spend. 'It's always $7 million; we don't know why but it is', Nield chuckles.

The deficit is tweaked back to zero every year, through weeks of negotiations, discussions and balancing acts that include the input of every senior manager in the company. As Maunder says: 'There is too much knowledge in this company for anybody to think they have all the answers.' The final decision rests with OA's artistic leadership— Collette, Hickox and Maunder—which keeps tweaking until the figures balance.

Each year, at the annual launch of its new season, OA presents patrons with answers to the seven-million-dollar question. They don't always draw universal applause, but the thought and care that go into them acknowledge the enormity of what's at stake.

Left: Spotlight on the score of *Carmen* during coaching for the 2005 season.

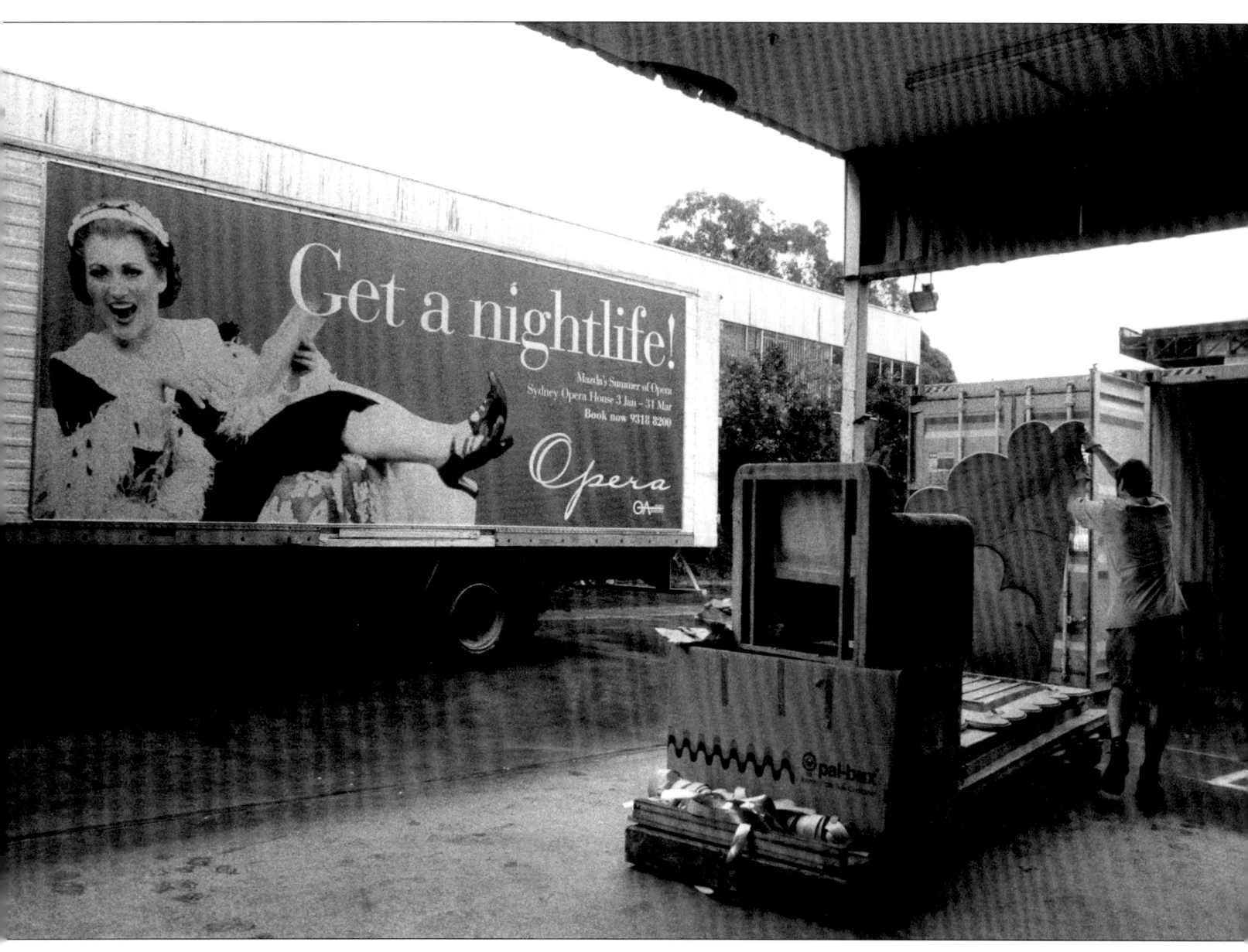

CHAPTER THREE

ATTRACTING AN AUDIENCE

Sales staff at OA's Surry Hills headquarters sometimes sing to customers on the phone.

More often, they make connections like 'It's the tune from the British Airways commercial', or 'Pavarotti sang it at the 1990 World Cup final'.

The point is that, singing or talking, staff bend over backwards to accommodate customers. And with good reason: each year OA has to sell 300,000-odd seats to about 230 performances in Sydney and Melbourne. Ticket sales account for 55% of the company's income and to ensure its survival, they have to grow by 5% annually.

Market research

Marketing and communications director Liz Nield and her team have developed the trade to a fine art, of which breaking into song is only a small part. Their skill is based on knowledge, in the first place of their patrons: Sydney and Melbourne opera audiences are well educated, with 31% holding degrees and 25% post-graduate qualifications, and they fall into the A/B income group. Although attendance increases with income, education level is the most reliable predictor of enthusiasm for the art form. The mean age for a single-ticket buyer is 45 and that for a subscriber 55—the same mean ages for these categories of ticket buyers twenty years ago, which suggests that the audience is regenerating itself. If its members are older, it's because tickets are expensive—opera lovers have to get through mortgages and school fees before they can indulge their passion.

Left: Soprano Amelia Farrugia sings opera's praises: the truck that transports sets between Stores, the Opera Centre and the Sydney Opera House serves as a mobile billboard.

Rather than regularly increasing ticket prices, OA expands box office revenue by boosting the frequency with which existing patrons attend performances, and by attracting new enthusiasts. The idea is to increase the number of people attending each performance, since the company is already performing as often as it can.

Tickets are sold in the first instance to subscribers, who comprise 40% of the company's Sydney audience and 50% of Melbourne's. Bucking international trends, OA has expanded its subscription base in recent years—it grows by 5–7% annually, with a retention rate of almost 80%

This is thanks partly to the efforts of subscriptions managers Craig Thurmer (Sydney) and Stephen Joyce (Melbourne). About a year before a season is announced, Thurmer, who joined the company in 1990 ('I am forever threatening to get a real job', he jokes), and Joyce, a part-time screenplay writer who came on board in 1997, compile the company's subscription packages.

They are built on OA's five different customer profiles, each of which comprises roughly 20% of the audience. 'Protectionists', in Joyce's words, 'don't see anything unless it's set before 1820 and costumed for it'. These viewers enjoy going to about thirty well-known operas, avoid both daring interpretations and contemporary operas and are ambivalent about light opera. 'Classical Traditionalists' accept that the company has to innovate and will experiment with mild new versions of old favourites, but avoid radical visions. They are prepared to give light opera a chance. 'Modernists' favour 20th-century opera like *The Love for Three Oranges* and *Billy Budd,* and will not go to much else. 'Conformists' relish daring new productions of traditional operas like *La bohème* and *La traviata* and love operetta, but they will not see anything from the 20th century or later. 'Modern Traditionalists' will see almost nothing but light opera and provide packed houses for productions such as *The Mikado* and *The Gypsy Princess*.

When putting together packages, Thurmer and Joyce weave the needs of all five categories into the deals on offer. People tend to become more adventurous with experience, but it can take years. 'You'd love for audiences to see a *Madama Butterfly,* then try a *Marriage of Figaro*, then move on to *Nabucco*, but it takes a long time', Joyce says. 'People are conservative when they're spending one hundred bucks.'

When packages have been finalised, each one is slotted into a particular day of the week—patrons like the regularity of having the same night of the week reserved for opera. They also enjoy going out during the day, which partly explains why matinées sell out first.

Staying in tune

Joyce, Thurmer and their respective sales teams sell subscriptions for ten to sixteen weeks after a new season has been announced. Since buyers like discussing their options and sometimes request to hear tunes, the telephone is their most important sales tool. Knowledge of the repertoire is essential. 'People will call you up and say, "What shall I see?", and you have to steer them in the right direction because if they have a bad experience they won't come back and they'll tell everybody else', Joyce explains. Thurmer spends two weeks training staff each year, giving them music to listen to and discussing the operas on offer.

The Sydney Opera House: OA's biggest billboard.

OA's staunchest supporters subscribe to each of Sydney's thirteen productions twice (they want to experience the cast changes). Opera tends to be their only form of entertainment; they often come by themselves and sales staff know most of them by name. 'We've been speaking to them for years', Thurmer says.

Joyce does not consider himself a connoisseur, 'which is good because it means I can't patronise callers'. In his experience most of the audience aren't specialists either. 'They just love what they love.'

Sales staff deal with a range of complications. Joyce, who mockingly refers to himself as 'the yes-man', estimates that it takes thirty seconds to say yes and thirty minutes to say no to a caller. 'I cost that into my budget because if you keep the phone lines blocked while arguing, other callers become annoyed waiting to get through.' And once you've spent half an hour saying no, your caller is not likely to buy a subscription anyway. He tries to be accommodating because it works best and rigid rules only alienate people. If someone rings up to say they forgot to attend a performance, for instance, he tells them off nicely, then, if he can, puts them into another show. 'I know they'll remember that.'

Complaints—sometimes dealt with by the subscriptions team—vary widely. A traditionalist might have heard, for example, that the cast in a new production of a cherished opera is dressed in space suits. 'I'll say look, forget about the space suits, the singing is what's important.' His sense of humour has failed him only once: when an irate patron rang up and insisted that *Cenerentola* wasn't the real story of *Cinderella* because it didn't include the plot twists of the Disney version he'd seen on DVD the year before. 'He was going to come round and smack me in the nose, so I put him through to the

communications manager, who explained that the story of *Cinderella* comes from China and has 17,000 variations.'

Subscribers are the backbone of OA's support base. While they enjoy cost savings by buying a package, the draw card seems to be the sense of ownership that comes with having the same seat every time. Yet the company's viability depends as much on attracting single-ticket buyers, a fickle market affected by anything from elections to the weather. Since the trend is for people to buy tickets later and later, the phone lines remain open until the box office closes for curtain up.

Opera by numbers

For sales purposes, operas are classified according to the history of their popularity. The popular category comprises the 'top ten' as demonstrated by past ticket sales and tends to be the same all over the world, with some anomalies: *The Pearlfishers,* for example, is much better loved by Australian audiences than by their European and American counterparts, while *L'elisir d'amore* is a top ten opera in the UK but less popular in Australia.

Medium-popular operas are lesser-known works of the great masters—Verdi's *Don Carlo*—or the most popular works of lesser-known composers: Offenbach's *The Tales of Hoffmann* or Massenet's *Manon.* Sales predictions for medium operas are the trickiest, according to Liz Nield. A star in a crucial role may make all the difference: OA's 2004 season of *Norma,* for example, attracted a much bigger audience than expected. The production had great reviews and a star in Elizabeth Connell, and thanks to Joan Sutherland's success in the role, older patrons knew it well. By contrast, the 2002 new production of the medium-popular double bill, *Cavalleria rusticana/Pagliacci,* drew smaller audiences than anticipated despite a stellar cast—the production failed to capture the audience's imagination.

The least popular operas are usually artistically ambitious works that extend the experience of seasoned opera-goers yet rarely create fireworks at the box office—Stravinsky's *The Rake's Progress* or Britten's *The Turn of the Screw.* They are budgeted modestly and usually perform accordingly.

The three types of operas are marketed in different ways. Popular works get big advertising campaigns, because someone browsing the Saturday entertainment section of a newspaper is far more likely to respond to an ad for a crowd pleaser like *Carmen* than to one for a relatively obscure work. 'An opera that is not well known is best left to direct marketing and thoughtful articles in newspapers' arts pages', Nield says.

The same principle applies to 20th-century and contemporary works which, contrary to popular belief, do not attract younger audiences. Nield learned this lesson when she devised

Left: *The Magic Flute* on display at the Arts Centre: popular productions receive the bulk of the promotional budget.

a marketing drive to sell Barrie Kosky's 1999 Sydney production of Berg's *Wozzeck*. Posters were put up in the inner city and ads referred to the cult movie of the time, *Eyes Wide Shut*. 'It was designed to appeal to popular culture', Nield recalls. 'The problem was that the opera was not popular. It did not sell tickets. I dragged my friends along, some of whom were experiencing opera for the first time. What I achieved was to guarantee that they would never attend an opera again—the music was just too hard.' The reviews were great though, and OA regulars thought it was marvellous. 'But they would have come to *Wozzeck* anyway, through our direct mail campaign.'

The experience taught Nield that however innovative and refreshing an esoteric work might be, seeing it still costs a lot of money and the people most likely to take the risk of spending it are those with a long history of opera attendance. New audiences come to opera through the familiar gates of *La bohème*, *La traviata* and *The Magic Flute*—the great works that over the centuries have converted thousands to the art form.

In summer, the bulk of the company's single-ticket income comes from tourists. Melbourne's Arts Centre offers fewer performances of each show than the Opera House, where tourism boosts box office by 30%. 'Those sails on Sydney Harbour are our biggest billboard', Nield says. 'Even people who don't particularly like opera will try it because they want to experience the building.'

Craig Thurmer, who doubles as OA's Sydney box office manager (in Melbourne single tickets are sold through Ticketmaster), factors tourism into his planning. He routinely establishes when cruise ships are coming in, for example, and fine-tunes his strategy accordingly: if it's the QE2 he would put in a *Falstaff* rather than a crowd pleaser because QE2 passengers are likely to include buffs. Shipping companies often take a number of tickets and on-sell them to their passengers for a small cut.

Public holidays are also taken into account—on Valentine's Day, romantic operas like *Romeo and Juliet* and *Madama Butterfly* are hot favourites—and an old-fashioned sales strategy that still works is to invite a selection of taxi drivers along, tell them about a show and give them a great night out, so that they will mention it to their customers.

Alerting the media

If lesser-known works benefit more from thoughtful press coverage than from conventional marketing tools, OA national publicist Emma Williams has learned that journalists are interested in great stories irrespective of their origins. 'You may have a good story in a popular opera like *Don Giovanni* or *La bohème* as much as you may have one in an esoteric work like Handel's *Rinaldo'*, says Williams, who joined OA after a successful career in public

Right: Tenor Philip Langridge rehearsing *Death in Venice* with director Jim Sharman: big names automatically attract media attention.

relations that included stints at the Navy and Sydney's Powerhouse Museum.

She aims to have a story about every production in every major publication, radio music program and TV show. But sometimes she's pitching three operas simultaneously, when realistically a publication will only have room for one opera story at a time. In such cases she tailors her strategy to the needs of individual publications, offering each editor the opera (or the angle) that would most appeal to his or her readership. A big name to whom everyone wants to speak presents the opposite challenge: when OA announced that Philip Langridge was coming to Australia for its 2005 revival of *Death in Venice,* every arts journalist in Sydney and Melbourne wanted to interview him. No one got an exclusive.

Williams finds it easy to source stories since colleagues are forever dropping by her office asking if she's heard about this director or seen that costume. And while experienced arts writers don't need someone to ring them up and suggest angles, many journalists do prefer to be briefed. To make sure she knows what she's talking about, Williams never misses a full dress or 'general' rehearsal, or an opening night. She often throws in an early piano dress rehearsal, plus a cast change somewhere in the middle of a run.

Once the tickets have been sold, it's time to find reading matter to inform and entertain patrons. Opera-goers like to be told who's who and what's plotting. Publications manager Michael Pedersen, a former music teacher who joined OA in 1992 (he's had various roles at the company), works with design manager Linda Matthews, a fine arts graduate who started at OA in Wardrobe. Together they ensure that patrons have the information they require at their finger tips.

With their combined historical knowledge of the company, this talented pair compiles and designs the programs for OA's mainstage operas, its off-stage recitals and the annual yearbook it supplies to subscribers. When commissioned copy for these publications arrives, Pedersen verifies every detail, bearing in mind that the audience will do likewise: classical music enthusiasts have not failed to spot a factual error in a program since the time of Hildegard of Bingen. (Once, when Matthews accidentally swapped captions for a picture, hundreds of aficionados let her know that they'd noticed.) Opera lovers are nothing if not passionate about the art form they adore.

Yet in Australia, as elsewhere, opera companies operate on a knife's edge. The biggest obstacles to OA's continued existence, says Liz Nield, are price and perception. Given the enormous cost of producing an opera, ticket prices are unlikely to come down relative to the cost of living. It is possible to influence perception, however.

Changing the way people think about opera is the ongoing challenge that drives the marketing department.

Left: Tenor Philip Langridge rehearsing *Death in Venice* with director Jim Sharman, watched on by baritone Peter Coleman-Wright.

CHAPTER FOUR

THE COURTING GAME

It used to be possible to identify the tourists in the foyers of the Sydney Opera House by their shoes: if you were wearing a pair of sneakers, chances are you'd spent the day looking at the sights.

This is no longer so. These days locals, too, turn up for *Don Giovanni* or *Death in Venice* in a pair of jeans and a T-shirt, and in a crowd where—thanks to the informality of the visiting classes—Nike and Levi are as well represented as Jimmy Choo and Lisa Ho, they certainly don't have to feel that they're lowering the tone of the event.

Opening night is the exception. The audience who gets to see the show first is likely to include a sizeable portion of subscribers and sponsors who still express their sense of occasion in stilettos, lace and the occasional bow tie. In fact, the opportunity to dress up for a big night out with clients is often part of the incentive for sponsors' support.

Commercial courtship

OA typically derives 15% of its annual revenue from 'development'—at the time of writing, $4 million from corporate sponsors, $1.3 million from individual donations and $700,000 from fundraising events. It tirelessly courts new sponsors—it has to—but has learned to tailor its tactics to suit the needs of each potential benefactor. 'We are very specific about who we target and that's one of the reasons why we've had success', says marketing and communications director Liz Nield. Despite this approach, she still sometimes knocks on ten doors and gets ten nos. 'It can be very disheartening.'

Before approaching a potential sponsor, an arts company needs to identify what it

Left: Sydney's Town Hall dressed up for a night of fund-raising.

has to bestow in return. OA offers several possibilities: the prestige of being linked to one of Australia's flagship arts companies, the opportunity to display good corporate citizenship through supporting worthy causes like education and regional touring, and client entertainment opportunities offered by opening nights and other operatic diversions.

OA's Board of Directors plays a crucial role in targeting and approaching potential sponsors. 'If I were to ring the chief executive of a big company and say I'd like to see him or her, I wouldn't get in the door', Nield says. 'But [Board members] Robert Morgan or Julia King or Gordon Fell know these people and it's easy for them to get an appointment.'

Sometimes she gets the date, only to discover that the match was not made in heaven. Like the time a Board member took her to a Victorian gambling company. 'They were keen to be seen to be doing the right thing and they clearly had funds to invest', Nield remembers. 'But their market just wasn't the opera audience.' Very occasionally she does say no to a sponsor—she would not, for example, take money from a tobacco company.

Rebecca Cuschieri, who as OA's corporate development manager approaches many potential sponsors, says it's not necessary to be an opera buff to do the job, and that sophisticated musical tastes can in fact be counterproductive. Whether or not a sponsor comes on board generally hinges on the first experience of opera they and their clients have, and someone with rarefied musical tastes might encourage them to see *Death in Venice* or *Lulu* rather than *Pinafore* or *Don Giovanni,* which does not always have the desired effect. A qualified lawyer, Cuschieri started her career as development assistant at Bell Shakespeare before joining OA in 1998. At the time she'd only seen two operas. She has since embarked on a journey of discovery which, she says, puts her in an ideal position for steering sponsors in a similar direction.

Opera's heroes

OA's two biggest benefactors—or 'Hero partners'—are Mazda and Australia Post. Mazda has been sponsoring the company since 2002 and in 2006 saved Opera in the Domain, OA's annual free outdoor event in Sydney, by agreeing to sponsor it for three years. The Melbourne-based company has a two-fold reason for supporting OA: it gives it a presence in Sydney, while the link with an iconic Australian arts company adds lustre to its brand. Mazda has identified customers and dealers who take an interest in the art form, and OA involves them in suitable activities.

'The way to keep a sponsor on board is to provide exemplary service', says Nield. 'We treat them in a confident but respectful way and we'll do anything they ask for: if they ask us to jump through twenty hoops, we'll do it.'

Cuschieri and her team, known as 'the party department' ('It's a little unfair—we organise rather than attend those parties!' she laments) ensure that those on board receive top service. After opening night, for example, they might treat a major sponsor to a celebration with clients in the Northern Foyer. OA would take care of everything from liaising with the Opera House and organising catering to ordering flowers and creating an ambience with help from Props and Technical. Cuschieri would arrange for singers to meet the group, and make sure that they know a little about the business. 'The sponsor manages the guest list and we manage the rest', she says.

One thing sponsors will never influence is repertoire. 'We rely on the market and therefore many of the operas we put on tend to be sponsor-friendly anyway', Nield says. 'But they would never say they don't want things like swearing or nudity.' Sponsors sometimes choose to attend operas that feature particular artists, especially when they've been supporting the company for a while. And some do prefer the esoteric end of the repertoire.

Australia Post, OA's other 'Hero partner', sponsors the company's touring arm, **Oz**Opera, which also performs in schools. With a post office in every town Australia Post has a vested interest in flourishing rural communities, and small towns which offer their inhabitants excellent entertainment are less likely to lose them to the city. Furthermore, support for education is essential for a business that makes a living out of people writing and sending letters. And when **Oz**Opera arrives in town the local postmaster or postmistress gets to offer the mayor and local business leaders a great night out.

OA's association with 'Gold' partner Maersk Line dates back to the company's co-production of *The Marriage of Figaro* with Welsh National Opera in 2002. Maersk Line (then trading as P&O Nedlloyd) agreed to ship out the production (a deal worth $40,000 in freight) in return for tickets and acknowledgment. Since then the company has trucked all OA's sets between Sydney and Melbourne and taken care of its interstate and overseas shipping. It also provides discounted, specially developed containers for storing costumes and sets. Thus, entire productions are shipped to Melbourne, where they sit in a yard until required. OA rents out the space that has become available at its Alexandria warehouse in Sydney as a result of the arrangement.

Yvonne Kenny woos the audience at a fund-raising dinner and auction.

'Silver' partners ExxonMobil, Qantas and Commonwealth Bank have been supporting OA since the 1980s. ExxonMobil, for many years the company's principal sponsor, now subsidises the chorus and free community concerts of opera highlights in regional Victoria, performed in conjunction with Orchestra Victoria. For its part, Qantas provides cash, airfares and fare flexibility. Like OA, it is a national icon and sponsorship buys it access to OA's high-value audience as well as treats for its Frequent Flyers. The Commonwealth Bank demonstrates its corporate citizenship by subsidising tickets for high-school students. IBM, another silver partner, supports OA with hardware and computer expertise, and in return OA entertains its clients.

If corporate donors make business decisions about sponsorship, individuals are motivated by a sense of the community in which they wish to live. 'When I approach a sponsor I'll say, "this is what's in it for you", and they either want it or they don't', Cuschieri says. 'For individual donors it's all about emotion.'

Left: Coach driver Bob Dove helps Australia Post deliver the **Oz**Opera experience cross-country.

Patron with a passion

Retired businessman Fred Street, who approached OA in 1999 with a view to sponsoring an opera education program for high-school students, passionately believes in personal involvement: 'Writing a cheque is commendable and I'm certainly not knocking it, but involving yourself and giving of your time means more', he feels. Attending many of the events offered by the program he funds has enabled him to meet participating students, which has brought him 'pure joy'.

Street's idea was to draw in students from socio-economic backgrounds and geographical areas that made exposure to opera unlikely, and to give them an unforgettable experience. Singer/teacher Victoria Watson developed the OperaEd program in consultation with him and the first group of students participated in 2000. The emphasis is on offering the teenagers a good time rather than on 'trapping' them into liking opera. 'If that happens, fabulous, but it's a bonus', Watson says.

Each year she approaches eight Sydney schools (around 1000 students participate annually). Initially she found it difficult. 'Schools constantly have people knocking on their doors with proposals. When we first started, most of the teachers had never been to the opera. So you'd ring them up and say, "I'm from Opera Australia", and they'd say, "Who's that?" It took a fair bit of negotiating to get it all happening.'

Once agreed, the first step is to send teachers a kit to prepare the students. Then she runs a school workshop day with fellow singer Murray Dahm. They encourage the youngsters to act out scenes, sing themes from the chosen opera and try on costumes

('They take hundreds of photos!'). A week later the budding buffs visit the Opera Centre, meet the singers, attend rehearsals and explore Wardrobe and Workshop. At the end of the day they go to Rossini's Cafe on Sydney's Circular Quay for pasta and harbour views, and then they're off to see the show. Like Cuschieri, Watson and Street choose operas 'with big emotions, love and death, blood and guts', for maximum appeal.

Street pays for everything, including A Reserve seats. Watson recalls describing the program to delegates from thirty-odd opera companies at a conference in Toronto. 'They were baffled', she laughs. 'Many of them had excellent education programs, but nowhere in the world was a private patron paying for kids to sit in A Reserve seats!'

Like Street, silver partner Douglas Mitchell has been supporting OA since 1999. Mitchell, inspired particularly by Elke Neidhardt's *Tannhäuser* and Moffatt Oxenbould's *Madama Butterfly,* has sponsored OA's productions of *Capriccio* (2000), *Tristan und Isolde* (2001) and *Lulu* (2003). Based in London and Melbourne, he and his wife Monica continue to support the company.

Gold partner Philip Bacon, proprietor of Philip Bacon Galleries, has been one of OA's most generous individual donors over the past fifteen years. 'Philip loves opera and believes in the company', Cuschieri says.

While OA boasts some longstanding partnerships, neither private nor corporate sponsors can ever be taken for granted. It was a blow when Seven Network, which had invested $14 million over a period of seven years, left the fold. In Australia there has not been an arts sponsorship of that size since. 'We don't resent them for pulling out because they had no obligation; they had their own business issues and they helped us to set up many of the things we do', Nield says, adding: 'If you keep a sponsor for three to five years, you're doing well.'

She is not optimistic about the future of arts sponsorship in Australia. 'I don't see any evidence of a philanthropic tradition emerging', she says. In fifty years' time, she suspects, OA will be funded in more or less the same way as now: through box office and subsidy. American opera companies survive thanks to corporate sponsorship and private donations because there are more Americans to make contributions, and more wealthy ones to make big contributions. In Australia, competition for the philanthropic dollar is fierce: children's cancer, sport, the environment—they're all worthy causes. 'When you have a small population, you get a small part of its generosity. You get the arts lovers.'

Adrian Collette, who takes the long view, does see OA gradually moving towards the American philanthropic funding model. But a profound shift in thinking needs to take place first.

'In America it's not only the rich who give', he says.

Right: Blacktown Girls' High student Kate Grgich eyes her headgear in the mirror. She participated in 2005's OperaEd program, sponsored by Fred Street.

CHAPTER FIVE

SONGBIRDS

'So what else do you do?'

It's a question that opera singers frequently hear. After more than two decades in the industry, countertenor Graham Pushee has accepted that even people who regularly attend opera rarely appreciate that training and maintaining a voice, learning a variety of roles and rehearsing a dozen productions a year is a full-time job. As bass-baritone Bruce Martin puts it: 'I don't know how many times I've been told: "You're lucky, you have a voice." To that I say: "Lleyton Hewitt is lucky, he has a tennis racket."'

Martin returned to singing in 2001 after two years supporting his wife following her diagnosis with cancer. He rebuilt his career by covering for other singers, memorising ten major new roles in fifteen months. Between rehearsals for OA's 2001 Melbourne production of *Batavia,* an extremely challenging work ('Richard Mills does not like repeating himself— every bloody bar in this opera has a different time signature!'), he was learning roles in *Lady Macbeth of Mtsensk*, *The Tales of Hoffmann*, *Faust* and *The Marriage of Figaro*.

Such feats of memory and endurance are essential attributes for singers, who are expected to arrive at the first rehearsal word and note perfect, their role memorised and a variety of different interpretations considered. The process can take anything from three to eighteen months. A new production is given six weeks of rehearsal; a remount a month. A singer can then expect to perform around eight performances of a show.

Small wonder that OA conductor and repetiteur Andrew Greene says: 'You don't choose to be a singer because you like doing it; you choose it because it would be just death otherwise.'

Hard slog alone does not even guarantee success. When asked what a singer requires for a successful career, Graham Pushee, who besides being a countertenor also acts as agent for other singers, responds with: 'Oh, everything!' In addition to having a fantastic voice,

Left: French language coach Marie-Claire illustrates articulation to a singer.

good looks, excellent training and the ability to work extremely hard, that means patience, ambition and being in the right place at the right time.

The right voice

Before they can locate the right place, singers need to find the right voice. For some it's as simple as establishing a voice type, for others it means identifying a preferred musical period or style. A singer may also grow into specialising in the work of a particular composer.

Welsh tenor Dennis O'Neill identified the repertoire that suited his voice while on tour with the State Opera of South Australia (SOSA) in the mid-1970s. The company's music director heard him perform in the UK and subsequently invited him to join the fledgling Australian organisation. 'They needed a house tenor they could afford and at the time I was very cheap indeed', O'Neill recalls.

After two dozen country performances of *La bohème* with SOSA, he discovered that temperamentally he was 'a Latino'. 'You can only put heart in your music if your repertoire suits your nature', he says, and white wigs and restrained gestures did not tally with his. He returned to Europe, obtained a scholarship to study vocal technique in Italy and became a Verdi specialist. Thereafter, when he cracked his high notes, 'at least it was in the right repertoire!'.

Yvonne Kenny didn't consider a career in opera until after she'd completed a degree in Biochemistry and Microbiology. Yet like O'Neill, the soprano found her voice with relative ease—at the age of 11 she sang Mabel in *The Pirates of Penzance* with all the high notes in the coloratura. Finding a niche came easily to mezzo-soprano Catherine Carby too: she'd been training as a soprano at the Canberra School of Music when one day her teacher announced: 'You're a mezzo.' Carby went home and researched the repertoire she would be singing. She discovered that she loved the characteristic mezzo roles of 'hags, bags, bitches and somebody's son, or somebody's mum'.

The process was more complicated for Angus Wood. His voice had a dark quality that made the baritone repertoire seem a logical choice when he was in his 20s, even though he never had trouble singing high notes. When training improved his top notes, former OA music director Simone Young suggested that he might be singing the wrong roles. She cast him as Cassio (a tenor part) in OA's 2003 production of *Otello*.

Wood lost ten years of repertoire when he switched voice types but is philosophical about it: 'I was repeating myself and it was time to learn new roles.' He found it difficult to establish his new status at OA, however, since for a long time the company continued to regard him as a baritone—after all, it had cast him in dozens of baritone roles. So Wood obtained a scholarship to the University of Michigan in Ann Arbor where he spent two

Right: Graham Pushee's voice type is often required for baroque opera. Here the countertenor rehearses for *Rinaldo*.

years doing a Masters. This enabled him to take singing lessons in an environment where there were no preconceptions and he could prove himself as a tenor. These days, overseas audition panels have difficulty believing that he was ever a baritone, although locally he is still sometimes asked to depict scoundrels and toffee-nosed fathers—typical roles for the darker male voices. He turns such offers down because both technically and psychologically it would be very difficult to alternate between voice types.

Tenors have traditionally been cast as romantic heroes because the unusual quality of their voices makes them stand out. The higher voices—tenors, countertenors and sopranos—sit above the orchestra, making them easier to hear. While baritones sometimes become tenors (Enrico Caruso and Plácido Domingo both did), the reverse seldom occurs. Because the high male voice is the exception rather than the rule, says Wood, a singer only trains as a tenor when his voice range has clearly identified him as such. By contrast, if you take ten men in a coffee shop, eight of them would be baritones—it's the average male voice. A male singer who is uncertain of what he is, therefore, would probably start with baritone repertoire.

Like many countertenors, Graham Pushee was originally a baritone. After his voice had broken he experimented with a range of voice types, until his teacher suggested that he train as a countertenor. When he sang the baritone repertoire, he remembers, it sounded as if he was trying to 'produce' the sound, whereas as a countertenor he created a natural, healthy vibrato.

Countertenors usually specialise in baroque repertoire, in roles originally written for castrati. They are probably the closest to the castrato voice that modern audiences can expect to hear, and like their predecessors they have surprise value. 'Some people laugh during a performance, some are shocked and some never recover', Pushee says.

Baritone Anthony Warlow had no trouble identifying his voice type—for him, as for Dennis O'Neill, the issue was choosing a suitable style. As a youngster he had a burning ambition to be in music theatre, but when he was 16, his father took him to see *The Magic Flute*. 'I loved it so much that I vowed I would play that role, in that costume, in that production.' Five years later, at the age of 21, Warlow was Papageno, in John Pringle's costume, in the 1984 remount of John Copley's production for The Australian Opera.

Richard Bonynge, who offered him the role, had no illusions about his voice. Warlow recalls being summoned to the maestro's room where, having sung a few scales, he was offered a position with the company: 'It was all very frightening, but Richard said, "Oh my dear, you're a marvellous young actor, you mustn't worry about the singing!".' It was not exactly what Warlow wanted to hear but it inspired him to try to create a character rather

Left: Yvonne Kenny has built a career in lyric soprano repertoire.

than attempt to impress with a voice that still had a long way to go. Since then, the vocal and language coaching offered by the company has helped him to build a technique which has stood him in good stead.

When several years later he decided to leave The Australian Opera to do a commercial run of *Guys and Dolls,* Moffatt Oxenbould encouraged him to broaden his horizons, reassuring him, 'and this was the greatest thing he said to me', that he would always be welcome at the opera company. Warlow has returned many times—he loves working with OA 'because of the sense of dignity and classicism that working with the company offers'. Musicals, on the other hand, taught him 'pizzazz and knowingness', elements with which he infuses his operatic roles.

The dynamics of opera

Andrew Greene, who has conducted widely in both genres, says an opera voice needs more control, a bigger range and a greater set of dynamics than a music theatre voice. On the other hand, a music theatre singer requires more energy and dynamism as a performer ('Opera has much to learn from music theatre in this respect') and is more likely to be expected to look the part.

Another difference between the genres, says Greene, is that music theatre singers use microphones while opera singers use their bodies to project sound. 'Hearing the unamplified human voice ride over large orchestral forces is what opera enthusiasts find thrilling and a microphone, which puts small and big voices on an equal footing, spoils the fun.' Amplification also tends to reduce a performance to a straight line, whereas dynamic contrasts are fundamental to classical music. 'It's about creating lows so that the peaks, when they do come, seem extraordinary.'

Nowhere is the divide between classical and popular styles of singing more evident than in the use of vibrato. In opera the technique gives sheen or sparkle to a tone and it can be essential. For example, if string players use vibrato to produce a warmer sound (as they might do in music from the romantic period), a singer who uses a 'white' or 'pure' tone against it will have difficulty being heard. Certainly some classical singers use white tone, particularly those who specialise in renaissance and baroque repertoire. Yet, classical singers who venture into pop, says Greene, find it almost impossible to switch the vibrato off even though the technique does not suit popular styles of singing. Opera singers who 'cross over' also tend to have trouble turning down the decibels when they sing into microphones. Correspondingly, music theatre singers venturing into opera can sound forced when trying to make themselves heard.

In short, while both disciplines require great skill, the golden rule for singers, Greene concludes, is 'to stick to what you do well'.

Which makes the apparent ease with which Warlow and fellow popular singer and tenor David Hobson move between styles all the more admirable. Hobson thought he'd found his niche—as singer and composer of pop music—when the Victoria State Opera offered him the role of Rodolfo in a 1987 touring production of *La bohème*. 'At the time I didn't know what Rodolfo was, or *La bohème'*, he recalls. 'High Cs didn't mean anything to me either.'

He was offered the same role in Baz Luhrmann's 1990 production for The Australian Opera. By then he'd been an ensemble member for some time and had decided that opera was not for him. 'There was so much to learn and I was a bit behind the eight ball.' But Moffatt Oxenbould asked him to meet with Luhrmann before he made a final decision. Director and singer hit it off and the *La bohème* production they did together became one of The Australian Opera's biggest successes, a feat of which Hobson is 'pretty proud'.

At the time he took the accolades for granted, yet today he appreciates that filling a two-thousand-seat theatre 'with luscious tones' requires a great deal of 'practice, heart and nous'. Although he still sings pop, he draws the line at rock 'n roll. 'As a rock singer you learn to scream, whereas in opera you have to contain that scream and make it beautiful. I couldn't do Judas in *Jesus Christ Superstar* now.'

Fledgling careers

A singer who has identified a niche next needs to hone his or her musical skills. One of the best ways to do so is through an opera company's young artists' program. OA offers an apprenticeship program for musicians on the brink of operatic careers, and each year a few lucky young artists (not necessarily singers) are invited to join its ranks.

Catherine Carby loves the 'hags, bags, bitches and somebody's son or mum' which, as a mezzo-soprano, she is frequently required to represent.

These artists have usually trained at a conservatorium or an opera school and have some performance experience under their belts. OA uses them in small roles and as understudies while they study Italian, French and German with the company's language coaches. They also receive instruction in acting, dancing and musical interpretation. Before these programs were introduced, some singers found their way into opera companies via the chorus—Angus Wood gained early experience this way. 'It was an escape from telemarketing and washing dishes', is how he remembers his days as a chorister at both the VSO and The Australian Opera. It was also an opportunity to learn by observing established singers.

Early public appearances can be crucifying for young singers, which is why OA offers them the opportunity to gain performance experience with its touring arm, **Oz**Opera, which appears in smaller regional venues. Dennis O'Neill is grateful that he was given the chance to 'try it out' away from the crowds. 'SOSA had the good sense to send me to the country rather than allow me to perform in town, but I'm surprised they hired me at all—I certainly wouldn't have!' he quips.

Angus Wood had to audition to be accepted into the chorus, but once there he was offered roles on the strength of previous performances. When he started freelancing, however, auditions were once again in the offing. He sums up the loathing these events inspire among singers and the repetiteurs who accompany them: 'I can't stand them—they are not recitals; they're not performances, and sometimes panel members read the paper while you sing.'

Catherine Carby, who seldom auditions these days, was 'never really a fan' either. She learned to go in prepared and to shrug it off when she didn't get the job—'which is hard when you're desperate'. She's not sure how much a panel can tell from an audition anyway. 'In theory if ten mezzos turn up the best singer will get the role, except that some people don't audition well, while others who do may not perform well.'

The idea of auditioning for former OA artistic administrator, Sharolyn Kimmorley, so unnerved baritone Teddy Tahu Rhodes—a Christchurch accountant at the time—that he stood her up. 'It takes my breath away to think of it now', recalls the singer, who has since achieved success at some of thew world's leading opera houses. Kimmorley was in Wellington, New Zealand, for a performance, and OA had arranged for Rhodes, who'd been recommended by a fellow singer, to fly there. He never made it to the airport, instead remaining at his desk in Christchurch where he locked the door and took the phone off the hook. 'It was absolute angst', he says. 'I knew I was supposed to be somewhere else and someone was waiting to hear me, and that the consequences of not having turned up were going to hit me from all angles.'

Left: What tenors do best: Angus Wood romances soprano Miriam Gordon-Stewart in *Fledermaus*.

Right: One of the most recognised faces of OA: tenor David Hobson, photographed from the wings during a performance of *Trial by Jury*, is at home in both operatic and popular repertoire.

He doesn't remember how he re-established communication with the outside world, but he found the courage to ring Kimmorley in Sydney the next day and ask her for another chance. Two days later he flew to Australia under his own steam and auditioned for Kimmorley and Moffatt Oxenbould. It did not go smoothly. 'They'd asked me to bring some *Figaro*, which I took to mean *The Marriage of Figaro*, but they had *Barber of Seville* in mind. I didn't know a single aria from it.' Nevertheless Rhodes was offered the role of Dandini in OA's 1998 *Cenerentola* revival.

Auditions are not only disliked by singers, they fill the repetiteurs who accompany them with dismay. A pianist may know in advance which repertoire to prepare, and occasionally may even have time to rehearse with a singer, but all too often repetiteur, artist and score meet for the first time at the audition. Although repertoire usually consists of music most repetiteurs know, younger singers tend to favour contemporary pieces which can be a nightmare to sight-read. It is small wonder that OA repetiteur Stephen Walter describes himself as a 'nervous Nellie' when it comes to these events. 'It's such an important occasion for the singer, but if you've had no time to prepare for it, it's very difficult to make a positive contribution.'

A repetiteur who is given time to prepare, on the other hand, is likely to spend hours practising music that will never be performed: audition panels, though they usually ask artists to demonstrate their range by bringing along several pieces, will seldom ask to hear more than one of them.

Learning the part

When an audition is successful, the next step is to memorise the role in time for the first day of rehearsals. How long this takes depends on its length and difficulty, and of course on the singer concerned.

For Yvonne Kenny language is the starting point. The three months it took her to learn *La voix humaine* for OA's 2005 Melbourne production was preceded by six weeks spent translating the text. 'I can't memorise anything unless I'm very clear about exactly what I'm saying', she says.

She learns the music with the help of a privately hired repetiteur (most freelancers do), even though she plays the piano herself. 'As a singer you have enough to concentrate on.' She works on it every day, taking a break every two hours. 'It's an incredibly long and detailed process and it's far more difficult to memorise text than music', she says. Once this is done, she starts working on interpretation. She enjoys researching her characters and says the opportunity to learn is one of the joys of a career in opera.

Dennis O'Neill, who had 107 roles in his repertoire the last time he counted, is at a stage in his career where he rarely learns new ones. His preparation for a role depends on when he last sang it—two weeks' rehearsal is sufficient if it has been in the last year. To keep things interesting though, he goes over the score and finds something to do differently—a diminuendo on a high C, for example. 'I enjoy inventing hurdles for myself', he chuckles.

Many established singers baulk at the thought of spending months learning music they may only perform a few times, so contemporary opera is often the domain of young artists hungry for exposure. Baritone Michael Lewis, who sang principal roles in John Haddock's *Madeline Lee* (Sydney 2004) and Richard Mills' *Batavia* (Melbourne 2001; Perth 2004; Sydney 2006) is an exception. 'After thirty years of singing you get tired of repeating the same repertoire', he says.

Lewis finds memorising complicated rhythms the most taxing aspect of learning contemporary music—pitching is easy by comparison: 'You can play Armageddon around me and I'll be able to pitch my next note'. Technology has simplified learning, however. With *Madeline Lee* and *Batavia,* Haddock and Mills provided simulated, quasi-orchestrated CDs that, when popped into a computer, gave the general shape of the music plus the solo line.

Soloists find input from a living composer invaluable. Haddock, though a repetiteur at OA, never taught Lewis his part ('I can't cope with being told how to learn something') but he made a few alterations at the singer's request.

Lewis found Haddock had a tendency to drive the human voice to its limits. 'As a repetiteur he batters the bejesus out of the piano, making it sound like a full symphony orchestra! As a composer he writes such poignantly beautiful music that the ratchet is turned up emotionally, which can make his music extremely difficult to sing.' Lewis recalls a passage from *Madeline Lee*, where a particularly moving section was followed by three or four phrases set much lower than he could comfortably reach. When he explained to Haddock that he would not be able to give the phrases the weight of expression they needed, Haddock transposed them up a fourth.

In the case of Wagner, stamina rather than range or rhythmic complexity is the issue. *Die Meistersinger* lasts six hours and once the character of Hans Sachs has made his entrance in Act I scene ii, he's on stage for the rest of the opera, singing 80% of the time. Bruce Martin sang it in OA's 2003 remount of the work.

He built up the staying power by singing continuously. 'It's like practising for a marathon', he says. Once he'd memorised the role he started singing through it every day, five days a week, for a month before rehearsals started. Some days he would add another role at the

Left: Teddy Tahu Rhodes waits in his dressing room before going on stage as Escamillo in *Carmen*, one of the few romantic hero roles in the baritone repertoire.

end—Jokanaan from *Salome* for example—and other days he would add two: Jokanaan and the Flying Dutchman. 'By the time I'd finished that I had hardly any voice left at all'.

Martin needed every bit of the strength he'd built up. *Meistersinger* was performed at Sydney's Capitol Theatre, which had no stage air-conditioning. On most days the temperature was 30 degrees when he made his entrance, with five-and-a-half hours to go. Chorus members routinely had to leave the stage in the final scene because they were feeling ill from the heat. 'It was an ordeal', says Martin, who drank twenty glasses of water during each performance.

Academic qualifications

Despite their enormous contribution, singers are still sometimes considered a lesser species of musician. Angus Wood, who holds a Masters in Music from the University of Michigan, laughs heartily at the notion. 'The perception that singers are idiot savants who make beautiful sounds without necessarily knowing what they're doing is certainly there', he says. 'Obviously occasionally that's true. But some musicians are extraordinary despite not having had a lot of training—you can't fault the logic of instinctive, innate musicality.'

These days, however, most opera singers are highly trained. John Haddock points out that an opera singer's schooling requires four times as much energy and resources as that of an instrumentalist: every singer needs a vocal studies teacher, Italian, French and German language coaches, a repertoire coach and training in stage craft. No other musician is expected to make music while simultaneously concentrating on a foreign language, engaging in stage movement, paying attention to the stage manager and interacting with other soloists.

Stephen Walter, who holds a Bachelor of Music (Honours) from Adelaide University and worked as accompanist for various organisations before joining The Australian Opera in 1990, says some singers come to repetiteurs when they already know their parts, while others need a lot of help. He enjoys doing basic work with a singer because it helps him gain better insight into the music. Describing himself as 'the most fallible and mistake-filled musician around', he derives great satisfaction from being able to provide solutions to singers. 'After all, the reason we're here is to get those notes off the page and into the theatre.'

Right: OA regular, bass-baritone Bruce Martin, waits in the wings with chorus member Juan Jackson during *Nabucco*.

Back to the classroom

Although repetiteurs are not vocal teachers, they may be asked for technical input. Their most important role is to alert the singer to the broadest possible spectrum of interpretative possibilities, so that nothing will come as a surprise when the conductor arrives. 'Some singers are totally insecure and like working in a little vacuum and that's what gets trundled on and off the stage every night', Walter says. 'Others enjoy exploring.'

The language coach often attends sessions with repetiteurs. Since OA has many Italian operas in its repertoire, it has a permanent Italian coach, Renato Fresia-Verdino. At university in Rome he spent four hours a day standardising his diction because he aspired to be a newsreader. Fresia-Verdino ended up a civil engineer, however, and moved to Sydney in his 20s. As a member of the Dante Alighieri Society, he heard that the opera company needed an Italian teacher for its young artists' program. He's been with them since 1985: 'Opera is a bug and once it's bitten you it doesn't let go.'

French language coach Marie-Claire, a former opera singer herself, intended to stay in Australia for a year, but changed her mind on her first day: 'I arrived at Bondi Beach on the 15th of July, in the middle of winter, and I said: "I stay here".' She sang with various local opera companies before a tumour in her throat put a stop to her singing career. Moffatt Oxenbould asked her to become a language coach. 'It was like a second lease on life', she says.

Given their different backgrounds, it's not surprising that Fresia-Verdino and Marie-Claire have different approaches. While Fresia-Verdino used to worry about his lack of musical training, he's since decided that it's better for a language coach to listen to the sound of the words without getting sidetracked by rhythm and pitch. He believes good pronunciation is crucial to opera.

'Conductor Carlo Felice Cillario and I used to argue over what was more important, the words or the music', he recalls. 'He would say, "*La musica! La musica!*" and I would say "*No Maestro, le parole!*" The words came first, and then a Verdi or a Mozart wrote music to make them…ahh…heartbreaking.' Marie-Claire approaches the job from the opposite angle. 'To be a language coach you have to know the repertoire inside out, plus the culture, the period, the background and the history of a piece, and you have to understand vocal technique', she says.

Most of the operas that OA performs are sung in an archaic, poetic version of Italian, French or German, and so the coach's job starts—about a year before opening night—with helping the singer to translate the libretto. The next step is pronunciation. Marie-Claire reads the French into a cassette and phonetically marks the singers' scores. Surtitles enable audiences to follow the dialogue irrespective of singers' language skills (or lack thereof), but pronunciation is important because there are always native speakers in the audience and besides, most artists will work overseas at some stage.

Fresia-Verdino encourages singers to solve their language issues well before rehearsals start because once the director and the conductor arrive there are many things to consider other than nouns and verbs. To Marie-Claire, on the other hand, knowledge of vocal technique comes into play when the show progresses from rehearsal room to studio. 'When singers start moving around, everything falls apart', she says. 'You need knowledge of vocal technique to help them solve these problems.'

Left: Repetiteur Stephen Walter describes his job as helping singers 'to get the notes off the page and into the theatre'.

Performance anxiety

By the time rehearsals start, the spectre of opening night will be disturbing many a singer's slumbers. Almost every artist has some private ritual which, for the sake of sanity, is observed on days of major performances.

Anthony Warlow tries to refrain from speech. Talking can be more tiring on the voice than singing, he says, and even whispering does more damage than just shutting up. But while he has tried communicating via a chalk board on performance days, living with a family during long commercial runs has made this approach impractical—for musicals at least.

Teddy Tahu Rhodes starts focusing during the day, 'because you can't just walk on; you already have to be in the role when you go on stage' and it requires immense concentration, even for smaller parts. He no longer gets as nervous as he once did. Five minutes before he had to go on the Opera House stage for the first time he was ready to run away. 'I remember sitting on the horse on which my character made his entrance, saying to two chorus members who were flanking me, "What am I doing? Do I really have to go on stage at the Sydney Opera House?" They kept saying "You'll be fine, you'll be wonderful".'

Catherine Carby never panics on the day—she reserves nightmares for the week before. In the dream she's usually in the wrong opera. 'I turn up at the theatre and they say the tenor is sick so we're doing *Macbeth* instead of *Fledermaus* and I'll be Lady Macbeth. And I'm going, "But I don't know the music! I have no idea what's happening!".'

Yvonne Kenny designs her performance-day routine to get her on stage by curtain up in the best possible shape. She lists everything she needs to do—eat, exercise, study the score, do a vocal warm up, rest, be at the theatre two hours before the show starts—and meticulously follows these instructions. 'It eliminates the panic of falling behind', she says. After more than three decades of professional singing, keeping calm remains her greatest challenge.

Sometimes singers miss opening night because they come down with laryngitis, break their arms, damage their vocal chords, or go through any other number of crises. This is why OA insists that every performer has a cover.

For ensemble members understudying comes with the job and some singers opt for freelancing to avoid it. Catherine Carby does not mind covering, provided she wants to master the role and feels she can learn from the singer performing it. She says understudies need to be 'totally prepared'. 'When you watch a show in rehearsal you think, "Oh yeah, you just go from there to there", but when you suddenly find yourself on stage it seems too close, or too far away, and a chair is much lower than you thought it would be. It really is quite unsettling; you have to have nerves of steel to go on at short notice.'

While joining the ensemble brings understudying responsibilities, it also provides access to training and performing opportunities most artists would not otherwise have. Teddy Tahu Rhodes, Catherine Carby, David Hobson, Anthony Warlow and Angus Wood have all been company members.

Through force of circumstance, Graham Pushee has not. Yet he has never regretted his long freelance career, which has offered many advantages. In Germany he worked with singers who had been ensemble members for fifteen years, and to whom opera had become a job. They would complain about their pay package, grumble about working conditions and groan about the hours. Ensemble singers also have limited options for doing the same opera in a variety of ways, with a variety of singers and conductors. 'Being a freelancer is tiring because you have to travel to a different country, speak a different language, do things in different ways. But it forces you to stay open and flexible.'

Right: Baritone Shannon Foley is coached by Stephen Walter.

Special guests

OA goes out of its way to create circumstances that minimise the stress for freelancers so they can give of their best. Guest artist manager Kate Larkins makes the first contact to establish the availability of a prospective guest artist. Larkins studied viola at the Sydney Conservatorium and completed a post-graduate degree in Arts Management before joining OA in 1999. She has found her music background invaluable in dealing with artists and their agents. 'You need to have knowledge of the singer and the size of the role you're offering', she says.

But in Larkins' line of work the most crucial skill is an ability to negotiate. She approaches agents two or three years before an opera's scheduled performance date. If an artist has not performed with OA before, she asks for advice on fee structures from other companies who have employed them, or from OA's artistic leadership, who can usually give an opinion on the standard of the artist and the size of the fee. 'The important thing is to establish that you are not offering a singer more than they would normally get, because they will certainly tell you if your offer is below their expectation', she says.

Agents are looking after their clients' interests and therefore dealing with them has its moments. Some drive a hard bargain ('the ones from New York are particularly aggressive'), so that it is imperative to remain fair, reasonable and above all, calm. 'It's always better to negotiate by email as you can be caught off guard on the phone', Larkins says.

When approaching star singers, she makes it clear that OA is unable to match the fees paid by companies like Covent Garden or the Met. ('But we're not the only company that cannot afford to pay that much.') Instead, she 'hypes' the Australian experience, and the fact that most singers who come want to return.

Some stars are booked up so far in advance that it's pointless to approach them, while others baulk at the distance, which makes it impossible to work for other companies while they are in Australia. On the plus side, many artists want to perform at the Sydney Opera House; some like the idea of escaping the Northern Hemisphere winter, and others like to perform elsewhere while European houses are closed for the summer. Once a singer is contracted, Larkins negotiates the manner of payment and the currency in which they are to be paid.

About three months before a guest artist is due to arrive, travel co-ordinator Trish Burt starts making arrangements. Burt, who joined the company in 1992, became hooked on opera as a young tour guide leading overland trips between London and Kathmandu, when she had the opportunity to attend performances at the Bolshoi and the Kirov. Back in Sydney she worked in the tourist industry before joining the opera company.

Left: Marie-Claire and soprano Tiffany Speight (p. 59) work through *Carmen*.

Today she assists guest artists rather than holiday makers, but the principles are the same. If an artist has worked with the company before she may simply book a flight and accommodation, but new artists need to be briefed on what to expect. Burt procures visas for entire families, filling in the forms and dealing with the Department of Immigration. Sometimes there are obstacles—local Immigration does not recognise nannies as family members, for example—but no artist has ever been refused a visa.

Right: Tiffany Speight.

Guests who know the company well (especially expatriates) are almost on auto-pilot when they arrive. For others it's a foreign environment, particularly if they haven't sat on a plane for twenty-four hours before. They tend to arrive in a state of shock and often remain that way until their jetlag has subsided. An OA representative meets artists at the airport and the company provides a list of contact numbers. It also supplies a starter kit of groceries so there's something in the fridge for artists who find themselves wide awake at 2 a.m.. If an artist's first call is two days after arrival, a company representative will accompany them to the Opera Centre on public transport to help familiarise them with the system. Everyone, from young artists to eminent guest conductors, receives the same treatment.

Vocal development

Using international guest artists enables OA to offer audiences a wide variety of quality voices. For their own part many local singers go overseas to enable them to fulfil their potential. This is particularly important for artists who specialise in repertoire too expensive for OA to produce regularly. Lisa Gasteen, for example, whose forte is Wagner, must look elsewhere to make full use of her talent.

Singing careers often start with lyric repertoire before progressing into heavy, dramatic roles. 'You need years of technical development to reach the point where you can comfortably sing over big orchestras', Andrew Greene says. 'Usually the voice will progress from a lyric quality suitable for Mozart and Rossini to a sound fitting for heavier repertoire like Verdi and Wagner.' Voices don't always develop in this way, but singers like to push themselves into bigger repertoire if they can because often it's better paid.

Knowing the limitations of your voice, however, is crucial if you want a long career. 'Voices are a certain size and singers need to accept and maximise that, not force it', Stephen Mould cautions.

Bruce Martin has no trouble turning down unsuitable roles. 'You must never get caught up in wishful thinking because the last thing you want is to find yourself on stage in the middle of a show and realise you shouldn't be there', he says. He would love to sing *Don Giovanni*, for example, 'but audiences want to hear young singers in the role, not some old codger'.

Yvonne Kenny, who has progressed from Donizetti to Mozart, Handel and eventually to Richard Strauss, cannot see herself ever doing the big dramatic roles. 'I'm a classical lyrical singer', she says. 'I would die happily if I could sing *Tosca,* but I don't think I ever will.' Similarly, Teddy Tahu Rhodes, who admires fellow baritones Bryn Terfel and Peter Coleman-Wright, knows he is unlikely to perform the dramatic repertoire in which they excel. He is at ease with the kind of singer he is, however, and the repertoire that he can do.

Agents have played a crucial role in guiding his repertoire choices. Once he was asked to sing Sharpless in a UK *Madama Butterfly* production, and his agent declined without even running the request past him. 'I hadn't sung in the UK at the time and the feeling was that it would not be a good role for such an important debut. It was very good advice.'

Singers with international careers often have different agents for different countries. Bruce Martin thinks agents are unnecessary for singers who work solely in Australia. 'Everybody knows everybody here', he says. 'I prefer to deal directly with the people who employ me.' Australian opera companies won't hire him if they don't think he's suitable for the role, and no agent will change their mind.

No matter how much guidance a singer receives, sooner or later almost everyone experiences a vocal crisis. For Anthony Warlow it came when he was diagnosed with cancer and had to undergo chemotherapy. For four months he completely lost his voice, and when it came back it had acquired a very high, bright quality. 'Planes of the voice that had been out of reach before were now achievable', he recalls. 'It was just phenomenal, particularly for music theatre.'

Yvonne Kenny had a traumatic experience of a different kind when she first went to London, where she joined Covent Garden and became flavour of the month. In her mid-20s, she was inexperienced and had to learn an overwhelming amount of new repertoire. An unhappy relationship was the straw that broke the camel's back—she lost her confidence, got stage fright and developed a slight wobble.

Most people, when faced by an emotional crisis, don't have to face 3,000 people and be brilliant. 'But if you're a singer you have to get out there even when you feel like bursting into tears.' To make matters worse, she was in the *bel canto* phase of her career, so that vocally she was perpetually walking a tightrope of runs, trills and turns.

Kenny overcame the crisis by revisiting the building blocks of her technique. She considers herself fortunate to have been kept on contract by Covent Garden, whose management was aware that for a couple of years she was not developing in the way that she might have. 'They stood by me and I am very grateful for that.' She got back on track and never allowed a person to be a negative influence on her career again. 'These days a destructive element in my life would not last longer than a week!'

Left: Italian language coach Renato Fresia-Verdino demonstrates his home language to a Young Artist Program class.

Time out

Given the pressures they face, singers probably need time to relax more than most professionals. Kenny likes to exercise or spend time with family and friends. She enjoys walking on the beach and swimming in the sea, 'in a vain attempt to keep the weight down'.

Bruce Martin also relaxes by spending time with family, especially since he is so often away from them. He hardly ever goes out and doesn't have time for partying—he doubts many singers do. When performing, his life consists of rehearsals, shows and visits to the gym to keep in shape.

When he really needs a break he borrows his wife's cameras (photography is her passion) and goes for a walk. In 1999 she had a melanoma and when she recovered— against the odds—Martin insisted that she get the best photographic equipment available. 'Her other passion is for exploring and she now has a 4WD which she drives all over Australia to take a photograph. I join her whenever I can, which is hardly ever.'

When you're trying to take time out, being recognised at the supermarket can be a distraction. When *La bohème* was at fever pitch it was a little crazy for David Hobson—one of Australia's more recognised opera singers—with both teenagers and old ladies accosting him in the street. While he is still sometimes approached for his autograph, it has died down now: 'We cater to a small demographic.'

Everyone agrees that an international career in opera, with its constant tensions and disruptions, is not conducive to a stable family life. Anthony Warlow describes the music world as 'a very jealous mistress', and in the lives of successful artists, 'sometimes the mistress wins'.

Yvonne Kenny seems to corroborate this viewpoint when she says: 'I chose a life of travel over marriage and children and even though I think about it sometimes at this stage of my life, I know it was the right decision for me. I was born to sing and I could not have done both things well—something would have snapped.'

Graham Pushee devoted twenty-four years of his life travelling from city to city, since even European opera houses seldom have more than one role a year to offer a countertenor. For some houses it's closer to one role every three years. Pushee reached a stage where he loathed the thought of going away, so in 2002 he moved back to Australia. In the first couple of years he regularly returned to Europe to honour commitments there, but he started refusing new overseas offers. 'In most careers, there is some ideal that you never achieved', he says. 'There are such things in my life too, but they no longer seem that important. Some singers sacrifice everything for the sake of their art, but every performing life comes to an end. What are you going to do when you can no longer perform?'

Right: Henry Choo, a member of the Young Artist Program, puts his Italian studies to use while perusing *La Fiamma* during a rehearsal of *Death in Venice*.

For those who continue to pursue singing careers *because it would be just death not to*, OA is not a bad place to do so.

'The company has a heart', says Dennis O'Neill. 'And to me that is unbelievably important. The need for love, attention and security may be based on a personal inadequacy, but at my age, who cares? I need warmth and acceptance and I've found it at OA.'

It's what happens backstage that makes for a good or bad experience, he says, and behind the scenes at the Opera Centre, everyone from the Wigs and Makeup people to the dressers, the staff directors, the language coaches, the rehearsal pianists, the publicists, right up to senior management, has given him a good experience. 'Life is extraordinarily easy here.'

David Hobson had a more ambiguous experience. When he first started working for The Australian Opera he didn't feel accepted by older singers, who seemed to think he was somehow dodging his apprenticeship. He was aware that he was regarded with suspicion and was 'kind of hurt by it'. Nevertheless, the company was very proud of the run-away success of the *Bohème* production in which he starred and in the years since he has certainly put in the hard slog. 'I feel fine when I work with OA now', he says.

Teddy Tahu Rhodes was in his 30s when the company offered him his first major operatic role. He says he owes his career to it. 'OA took a huge risk by offering me the part of Dandini in *Cenerentola*, when it had no idea if I could sing coloratura.'

Yet OA has never asked him to do something of which he was not capable. 'They guided my career and they never stopped me from going away and doing something else, in fact they've encouraged and enabled it.' In less than a decade, besides becoming one of OA's star attractions, Rhodes has built an international career that continues to expand.

But such success stories are rare. When one considers the level of talent and application demanded of singers to realise the art form that Dr Samuel Johnson famously described as 'an exotic and irrational entertainment', and the frequency with which the best efforts lead nowhere, it's not unreasonable to wonder if it's worth the angst and heartbreak.

John Haddock, for one, has no doubt that it is. 'Shylock's speech, *Hath not a Jew eyes?*, can move an audience to tears in eighteen lines', he says. 'A singer can do the same in two words.'

Left: Tenor Dennis O'Neill and baritone John Bolton Wood backstage at *Tosca* in the Domain: O'Neill relishes the care and support afforded guest artists.

CHAPTER SIX

SENSE OF DIRECTION

David Freeman passionately believes in opera that engages with society in its time. 'If you care about the art form, ride it hard', says the Australian-born director of OA's productions of *Nabucco* (2005) and *The Magic Flute* (2006). 'Make it relevant for today—don't pamper it and don't clip it like a little poodle and colour it pink.'

When deciding on ways to present opera to 21st-century audiences, directors play a crucial role. In fact, many patrons now queue to see the work of star 'producers'—Peter Sellars and Baz Luhrmann—irrespective of who is singing or conducting.

Inspiration strikes

Once hired (usually eighteen months to two years before opening night), it is up to the director to come up with a bold vision. To do so, he or she might study the history, art, politics, TV or literature that relate to a particular opera. The director also appoints a set and costume designer, who helps to develop the concept for the show. About a year before opening night, the set designer builds a model to illustrate the idea to the company.

Some directors involve the conductor in the conceptual stage. Stuart Maunder, for example, considers 'major input' from the conductor essential for a unified vision. He had many discussions with conductor Andrew Greene when working on concepts for OA's 2005 production of the Gilbert and Sullivan double bill, *HMS Pinafore* and *Trial by Jury*.

As a rule though, conductors prefer to focus on musical details: the version of the work that is being performed, the cuts that are being made, the language in which it is being sung. If an established conductor distrusts a particular director, he or she would

Left: Stuart Maunder, flanked by French language coach Marie-Claire, directs *Romeo and Juliet*.

simply turn down the invitation to conduct the opera, as Richard Bonynge has done many times in his career. 'If I can't adapt to a director's ideas then I don't want to be part of the production', he says.

Taking the reins

When planning a new production there are as many approaches as there are directors. American director Francesca Zambello, whose OA credits include Shostakovich's *Lady Macbeth of Mtsensk* (2003) and Prokofiev's *The Love for Three Oranges* (2005), describes hers as a journey: 'You're the crew on a boat and the director is the captain, whose role it is to make sure everybody sails into the same port.'

For *The Love for Three Oranges,* she wanted to create 'a visually rich and fruity world' to reflect the outpouring of sound and colour in the orchestra. Prokofiev's music was partly a response to constructivism, a Russian artistic and architectural movement of the 1920s that 'constructed' abstract artworks from industrial material. Zambello and designer George Tsypin drew on this zany art to create a universe that reflected Prokofiev's score: there were giant oranges, crazy cacti and a seriously dangerous cook. Zambello set *Oranges* in the period in which it was composed, but there are other options: some directors choose the period in which the composer lived or the period in which he had set the work, while others may re-set the opera in the present.

When OA approached Melbourne Theatre Company artistic director Simon Phillips to direct its 2005 production of *La bohème*, his instinct was to update Puccini's crowd pleaser to the present. Phillips, whose credits for OA include *Falstaff* (1996), *L'elisir d'amore* (2001), *Lulu* (2003) and *The Merry Widow* (2004), says in an art form that demands a suspension of disbelief on almost every level, it's easy for a production to become 'this weird beast where people sing beautiful music to a loosely appropriate story'. He wanted to set the opera in the here and now so that the audience would connect with what was happening on stage.

He faced two obstacles: in the first place an update is risky and a company as dependent on box office as OA needs full houses for what is arguably the most popular work in the repertoire. Secondly, he had to contend with the legend of 'Baz's *Bohème*'—set in the 1950s and premiered in 1990, one of The Australian Opera's greatest hits.

Phillips found the spark he was looking for while watching a DVD of a traditional *Bohème* production. Whenever he paused the DVD player to make notes, his television set would switch to an intensely lit modern German film that was playing on SBS World Movies. 'The environment was brutal yet seductively colourful', he remembers. It was exactly the world he'd been trying to imagine. The result was a 21st–century, urban *Bohème* that turned Puccini's *verismo* style into a gritty social realism. Critical response to it was divided, but audiences loved it and it reached its box office target.

If the challenge for Phillips was *Bohème*'s established popularity, finding an angle for a piece with no production history and low box office expectations might seem a breeze by comparison. Yet when developing his concept for OA's 2004 production of John Haddock's new opera, *Madeline Lee*, Michael Campbell faced other obstacles. As co-writer of the libretto, he discovered that when directing the work he had to do 'a 180-degree flip from "in, looking out" to "out, looking back in"'. It was only when he'd settled into what he calls 'a director's headspace' that he was able to tackle the issue of finding a concept for the production.

Madeline Lee examined the esoteric theme of how humans construct reality, but Campbell also wanted to ensure that the audience stayed connected to the opera's compelling narrative. Brian Thomson's set for Belvoir Street Theatre's production of David Hare's *My Zinc Bed* sparked the idea of visually anchoring the story. Thomson filled *Madeline Lee*'s stage with a crashed B17 bomber which provided a powerful backdrop to the unfolding plot.

Director Francesca Zambello discusses proceedings with Richard Hickox during a rehearsal of *The Love for Three Oranges*.

David Freeman and designer Dan Potra's vision for their 2005 *Nabucco* production grew out of many ideas. 'British director Peter Brook once told me that you didn't want to start a production with a concept, but that you'd better have one by opening night', Freeman quips. 'Whenever somebody asks me what my concept for a production is, I think what a pity to have only one.'

A poster of Saddam Hussein that had appeared in *Time* magazine before the Iraqi invasion provided their inspiration: it portrayed Saddam as Nebuchadnezzar (Verdi's Nabuccco), riding a chariot but aided by modern weaponry. By mixing periods in a similar way, Freeman and Potra's production hinted that the ancient conflict remained unresolved 2,600 years later.

It was not the only concept that informed the production. When an opera is well written, says Freeman, the director's role is to work out what the composer and librettist are trying to say and then find a way to present it on stage. *Nabucco*, though it has musical energy and an exciting narrative, 'tells its story rather badly'. The reason is that the opera is more concerned with Italian politics in the 1840s and the struggle for unification and

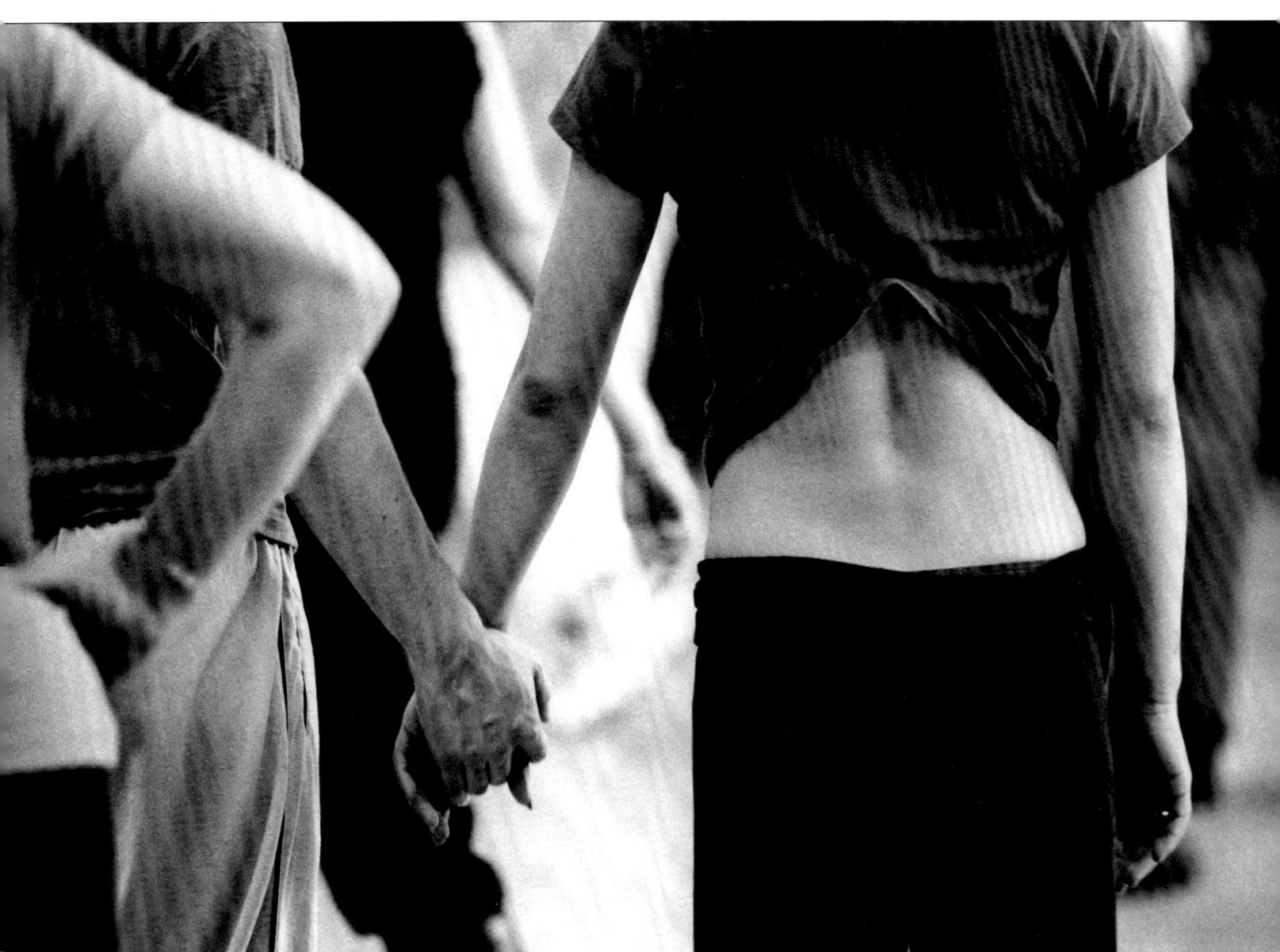

independence, than with presenting a gripping plot and convincing characters. Freeman therefore had to find a way to convey the work's political stance rather than its narrative.

To Verdi the exiled 'Hebrews' of *Nabucco* represented the Italian people of his day. To Freeman, although 21st-century Jews were in some ways synonymous with their ancient counterparts ('anti-Semitism is still rife'), in today's Middle East, Palestinians were the exiles. In a scene that encouraged the audience to consider the situation from both perspectives, he had the chorus—dressed as Jews in 1940—sing the famous 'Va'pensiero' lament from behind a wall that resembled both the ghetto walls of the Second World War and the wall separating Israel from the West Bank today, thereby invoking the Palestinian issue. To reinforce the point, as the last notes died away, Freeman had a child step forward and flick a Palestinian headscarf over the wall. He wanted to create debate, but says that the comparison was not meant to offend.

If Freeman's aim is to provoke discussion, Stuart Maunder and designer Roger Kirk's concept for *HMS Pinafore* and *Trial by Jury* sought to entertain and amuse. Maunder, known as OA's 'Mr Gilbert and Sullivan' ('Oh, how embarrassing is that!') admits that the British duo's works are 'a passion, almost a religion, which is quite sick', and that he still laughs at the jokes. *Pinafore,* a satire on a class-ridden society, offered endless possibilities for updating them. 'You think wisecracks about class are not quite Australia', Maunder says, 'but a glance at the social pages on Sunday makes you realise we do have social strata'.

Visually, Maunder and Kirk set out to reflect the work's 'prudishness and elegance', which led to a prewar, *Titanic* look reflected in grand hats, beauty and class. The companion piece, *Trial by Jury*, was set in a modern court of law and evoked the buzz of a very public divorce.

Since costumes for chorus members comprise a sizeable part of a new production's budget, levels of elegance and numbers of hats often require negotiation. Few directors know this better than Lindy Hume who, having directed *The Barber of Seville* for **Oz**Opera in the 1990s, was asked to direct the work for Houston Grand Opera (HGO) in 2005.

Setting a standard

Directing the same opera in different productions is 'a very nice challenge', Hume says. 'It's not as if I have only one version of an opera in me.' The **Oz**Opera production had a modest budget, operated with a small team and was designed to move around Australia.

Working with a different creative team provided a fresh perspective and HGO's sophisticated technology generated new possibilities.

Yet limited funds have never fazed Hume. 'Just because the budget is small there's no reason why the ideas should be small'. Her popular 1992 *Carmen* production for the West

Left: Cast members await direction in *The Love for Three Oranges.*

71

Australian Opera was produced on a shoestring. Moffatt Oxenbould acquired it for The Australian Opera, and it's still a classic in the OA repertoire.

But while acknowledging there's a time and place to be experimental and use emerging directors and designers, at a certain point, Hume says, audiences no longer want to see a 'cheap and cheerful' Baz Luhrmann (his Australian Opera *Bohème* was produced on a tight budget); they want to see the version that was staged on Broadway. She believes that OA should be the standard bearer of Australian production values: 'When you do a show for Australia's national company, you have every right to expect the standards you would find in national companies around the world', she says. OA's productions should present the Australian public with the opportunity to see 'the shiny, finished, high expertise of cutting-edge technologies and theatrical gestures', because if they can't see it at the Sydney Opera House or the Arts Centre in Melbourne, they're not going to see it anywhere.

Right: Director Simon Phillips in full flight.

Casting considerations

In an ideal world, once a gripping concept for the new production has been developed, suitable singers would be identified for key roles. In reality principals are often in place before the director has been appointed.

Directors are adamant that casting can make or break a production, yet practical considerations often exclude them from the process. Distance, for instance, made it impossible for Francesca Zambello to attend auditions for her Australian productions. After *Lady Macbeth of Mtsensk*, however, she had a fair idea of who was available so when Richard Hickox started casting for *The Love for Three Oranges* she spoke to him as well as to OA artistic staff about the kind of people she had in mind.

Zambello looks for flexible, creative singers who have something unique to offer. Although she does not expect everybody to have perfect size 10 figures, she likes to cast 'more realistically'. 'We're very much a visual society and opera reflects that now', she says. If many singers still don't look the part it is because there are operas—*Tristan und Isolde* for example—that only five people in the world can sing on an international level. 'You have to choose one of them and sometimes you have to make visual compromises', Zambello says. 'It's never worth casting somebody who can't sing the music.'

David Freeman agrees that casting is 'terribly important', even though he was not involved in casting *Nabucco*. He cites as proof the fact that casting his 2005 production of *Carmen* at London's Royal Albert Hall took two years. Simon Phillips says bad casting can ruin a production and affirms that opera companies often don't consult with directors in this regard.

Michael Campbell, who describes casting as 'about 70% of the job of a director', is the exception here because unlike his colleagues, he had virtual carte blanche when choosing singers for *Madeline Lee*. It was a new work and the company relied on the judgement of its creators, Campbell and composer John Haddock, a repetiteur at OA, who were conveniently stationed in Sydney. They tried to balance acting and musical ability with the right combination of singers. 'The drama of the work happens *among* the people on stage; it's not just a matter of finding the right fit for each individual role', Campbell says.

Even though new works have a better chance of taking flight if star singers launch them ('Especially if the star took off some article of clothing during the night', Haddock quips), *Madeline Lee*'s creators chose not to go this way because of the ensemble nature of the work. 'We felt one person's fame would unbalance the casting', says Haddock.

Director David Freeman (right) and assistant director Patrick Nolan give their full attention to a rehearsal of *Nabucco*.

The composer's challenge

Madeline Lee lived up to OA's box office expectations, but generally speaking new works are a huge risk and rarely do they find a place in mainstream repertoire. Francesca Zambello puts the situation into perspective when she says: 'In the year *La bohème* was premiered—1896—at least one hundred other new operas were composed. At the time no one knew *Bohème* would be the one to last the distance.' She feels that until recently, contemporary opera has been the domain of academics who seemed to compose for each other. 'And that really screwed us—people working in the business—and the general public.' But with works like André Previn's *A Streetcar Named Desire,* Jake Heggie's *Dead Man Walking* and Rachel Portman's *The Little Prince* now being performed around the world, new opera is once again becoming more popular.

David Freeman, who has commissioned many new pieces and worked with some of the world's foremost living composers, agrees that contemporary opera went through a stage 'where it was really not what people wanted to hear', leading to the creation of works he describes as 'squeaky door music'. But like Zambello, he senses a change in direction, represented by the work of, among others, Gyorgy Ligeti.

Freeman also sees possibilities for renewal outside the mainstream and favours encouraging first-rate pop composers, 'when they're about 35 and no longer hot in quite the same sense', to write opera. When The Who's *Tommy* and Andrew Lloyd Webber's *Jesus Christ Superstar* came out in the 1970s, he thought they represented a real possibility for exploring a new direction, and he still thinks it's an option worth pursuing. 'You have to be bold; you can't just go around singing the same tiny little bunch of operas; it's too depressing.'

Madeline Lee's composer, John Haddock, learned to write opera after years of coaching singers in the world's best-loved repertoire. He taught five- to eight-year-olds ('It was very good preparation for working in opera!') before joining the VSO and OA as repetiteur, and later spent a year as head of music at Dallas Opera. Although he has post-graduate qualifications in composition and conducting, he says it is his practical knowledge of the repertoire, coupled with insight gained from accompanying composer workshops, that taught him how to write for the medium.

'Some composers seem to think, "Oh I can write an opera, I've seen *Tosca*"', he says. But an opera composer needs specialised skills, including a highly developed sense of drama, an understanding of the role of the orchestra and knowledge of how composers of the past have solved dramatic problems. Many contemporary librettists, too, have lost the skills of their forebears, Haddock feels. 'At the end of the 20th century, the only people who seemed to understand how to marry words with music were folk and pop singers who had to stand up on stage and sing what they'd written—Don McLean, Joni Mitchell, Janice Ian, John Denver.'

The eminently singable phrases penned by troubadours like Don McLean (*American Pie*) are built on a system of subtle alliteration. Above all they are simple, Haddock says. When we can't hear what someone is singing, it's often because the words are too long. 'By the time the singer comes to the end of a three-syllable word, because of the extension of the vocal line the audience will be unable to remember what it is.'

Although there are no easy solutions, Haddock hopes that opera composers will create new scores in touch with musical and spiritual values, and pass their skills on to future generations.

Yet in the past half-century few new operas have found their way into mainstream repertoire, and opera companies have continuously recycled established works. This has contributed in large measure to the rise of the director, on whom the onus for 'making opera for today' now rests. As Zambello says: 'The score is the score—relating it to our own time is the job of the director or the producer, as we call them in the States.'

Taken to extremes—especially in countries where subsidised opera companies can afford to turn a blind eye to the box office—this has led to some bizarre productions, created in the spirit of what has been called 'produceritis'. David Freeman used to regard Germany, with its 80-odd state-funded opera companies, as paradise, but eventually he came to the conclusion that when ticket sales were an insignificant part of its income, a company started 'in a somewhat unholistic fashion' to perform for itself. 'There has been this extraordinary movement of directors who seem to think the most important aspect of a production is the critique it makes of the piece.' In Australia, where opera companies live or die by ticket sales, the more extreme strains of 'produceritis' have not taken root, although the importance of the director is undisputed.

On the rare occasions that the curtain goes up on a newly composed opera, the composer is subjected to as much scrutiny as the director. Directors who have worked with living composers agree that the process has to be collaborative.

Lindy Hume joined forces with composer Richard Mills and librettist Peter Goldsworthy for the premier of *Batavia* in 2001, and found the experience very rewarding. 'If you are lucky enough to have the composer and librettist still living', she says, 'what sort of fool would you have to be to say, "I'm going to direct it *my* way" when they have different ideas? It's my job, as director of the first production, to make sure that what is staged *is* what the composer and librettist had intended'.

Nevertheless, she ignored most of Mills and Goldsworthy's stage directions. 'They were the directions of a composer and a librettist', she says, smiling, 'and not all of them would have worked on stage'. Instead she sat down with Mills and discussed theatrically interesting ways to say exactly what he wanted to say. 'In opera it's never a case of "that's my idea" or "that's your idea" anyway—the best idea wins.'

Mills himself says an opera composer needs the courage to cut. He remembers chucking out pages and pages of music when going through the original piano score for *Batavia* with Hume. 'If you write for the theatre you cannot afford to be precious', he says.

A creator doesn't have the last word on a work anyway, says Michael Campbell. 'The score is like a recipe—you can have fantastic ingredients, but until you've cooked the dish, it's a recipe, not a dish.'

In David Freeman's experience, heavyweight composers—'Boulez, Glass'— have no qualms about adapting their own or other musicians' work to suit the requirements of the drama. He recalls trying to find a compromise with Boulez when they were doing a Ligeti piece in Paris once: 'I said, "Look Pierre it's very hard to get from here to there; there's very little music; is there any way you can play it a bit slower?" And he looked at the bars in question really closely and said, "You know, if I play that slower it's going to fall apart…but I could play it twice"'.

Surviving revivals

It is not only composers who have to let go of what they've written. Directors must also release their productions when they are revived. In a new production, the assistant director writes down every detail of the director's instructions, so that the show can be reproduced in its original form even if the original director is not available.

But a different director's take, however faithful to the original, is never quite the same. Lindy Hume has mixed feelings about having handed over her productions of *Carmen* and *Fledermaus* to revival directors in 2005. Mostly she feels relief. The original director can only develop and revise his or her concept within the parameters of the existing production, which means at a certain point it stops being a celebration of the original idea and starts becoming limiting. 'I'm ten years older now and not the angry young woman I was when I made *Carmen*', Hume says. 'I have different things to say.'

She never saw the 2005 revivals. 'Really, it's over—it has to be. It would be too weird to see the productions in other hands.'

Baritone Michael Lewis rehearses an entrance in *Nabucco*.

Some revival directors diverge widely from the original concept, with varying degrees of success. Hume feels a revival director should be able to follow their instincts without feeling inhibited by concerns that the original director would probably have done things differently. 'It becomes quite complicated, really.'

Somewhere between a remount and a new production are the so-called 'restudied' productions. Michael Campbell, who directed OA's restudied version of John Copley's 1988 production of *La forza del destino* in 1997, admits he's never quite managed to get his head around the concept of making a 'new production' using somebody else's set and costumes. 'All in all, a very difficult call', he says.

Despite its inherent difficulties, opera continues to attract top theatre directors. For Simon Phillips, the thrill is in the discipline. 'The difference between directing theatre and opera is like the difference between writing free verse and writing sonnets.' In opera, the music defines what a director can and cannot do, and Phillips finds this situation a brain tease. He also loves working with conductors.

David Freeman regards opera as a branch of theatre. He is fascinated by music, although

what he calls 'the big stand and deliver' bores him. He believes theatre's role is the public scrutiny of extremes. 'It's about being private in public; if you're being public in public you're just making speeches.' Yet in an art form as complex as opera, such exploration is difficult to achieve.

Today's audiences are too used to the casual realism of sitcoms and news bulletins to take dramas in which girls swap fiancés back and forth between breakfast and dinner seriously. Yet directors, working within the constraints dictated by the music, have to find ways to present the often bizarre plots in which some of the world's best-loved music is packaged.

Still, as Freeman points out, *Così fan tutte*'s plot is no more implausible than that of Shakespeare's *As You Like It*. And Michael Campbell feels it's unfair to bring the sensibility of the age of film, musicals and DVD to 18th– and 19th–century opera anyway, since it creates the perception that there is something wrong with the works. When Verdi wrote *La forza del destino*, composers and librettists were not concerned with 21st-century theatrical sensibilities. 'It's the job of the director to make the opera enthralling to a contemporary audience', he stresses.

Future directions

Some directors are more optimistic than others about the art form's ability to maintain a niche in a fiercely competitive entertainment environment. Freeman's dissatisfaction with mainstream opera prompted him to start his Opera Factory companies in London and Zurich in the 1980s, which became known for their 'radical chic' productions. Yet by the time these companies had become unsustainable, twenty years later, mainstream opera had not changed much at all: companies were still 'pandering to the wishes of the most conservative section of their audience', which was still 'guarding the clichés and conventions that keep 98% of the population away from opera'.

Freeman suspects the status quo is rooted in an operatic crisis of confidence, caused by the inaccessible musical language of the second half of the 20th century, which made audiences stay at home. The death of opera in translation, which reduced the text to 'a vehicle on which to float beautiful sounds', contributed to the dilemma, and on top of this opera singing is no longer generally understood and admired—pop has become the language of all generations. When an art form loses confidence in itself, he concludes, it tends to try to please its existing audience rather than to look for new audiences.

Francesca Zambello agrees that opera has the most conservative audiences of any art form ('and the ones who speak the loudest tend to be the ones who want to preserve

Left: David Freeman directs members of the cast in *Nabucco*.

the old rather than experiment with the new'), yet sees a lively future for the industry. Companies will keep reinventing old works while developing new ones, and technology will help bring further renewal. While some of us will always prefer the magic of live performance, DVD and future technologies will create new converts to opera, and to an increasing extent, studio productions will be tailored to these mediums. Zambello predicts that the internet will bring about an even more profound transformation. 'In time people will be able to log on to performances at the great houses of the world on a daily basis.'

Whether it's performed online, on stage or in the studio, opera's future will continue to be influenced by the way in which it is presented. For the foreseeable future, directors will play a pivotal role in its evolution.

Right: Repetiteur and composer John Haddock, in his role of rehearsal pianist.

CHAPTER SEVEN

MASTERS OF DESIGN

To designer Stephen Curtis, the creative energy and technical skill of the people who operate OA's manufacturing workshop are the company's greatest resource. 'This expertise is far more valuable than big budgets', says the man whose sets for the company include *The Turn of the Screw* (1987), *The Cunning Little Vixen* (1997), *Lulu* (2003) and *La bohème* (2005). 'If the talent and technical know-how are there, it's always possible to invent a more cost-effective way of realising a concept.'

Sets come into being through the efforts of many experienced, resourceful and devoted artisans, yet mobilising their energies requires the spark of a designer's idea. Dan Potra, who created OA's sets for *Carmen* (1995), *Ariadne auf Naxos* (1997), *Jenůfa* (1998), *Batavia* (2001), *Nabucco* (2005) and *The Magic Flute* (2006), says a design that takes a bold stance will come through. 'Even', he laughs, 'if the idea is bad'. In his opinion a production that fails to make the audience sit up and think is pointless.

He uses an anecdote to explain the need for controversy. When he and his family moved house in the run-up to OA's 2005 *Nabucco* production, his next-door neighbour, whom he'd invited for a barbecue, asked what he did for a living. Potra replied that he was a designer, which caused his guest to wonder which type. 'Theatre, opera, film…', Potra explained. 'Ah!', exclaimed the neighbour, 'a *useless* designer!'.

Potra insists he does have some use. 'It's true that what we do, though creative, is ultimately self-indulgent, but a production that encourages debate furthers the audience's sense of tolerance.' *Nabucco* aimed to achieve this by drawing attention to the complexity of the issues surrounding the conflict in the Middle East.

To Potra a good design incorporates many ideas, and *Nabucco*'s set included several

Left: Designer Roger Kirk and design assistant Robin Auld unveil the model for *HMS Pinafore* at a design presentation.

secondary concepts to support its main theme. One of the most striking was a wall that exploded at the end of Act I and provided a metaphor for conflict erupting like a festering sore.

Potra grew up in Romania and settled in Australia in 1988 ('Chernobyl frightened me and I was madly in love with the swimmer Shane Gould, whom I still haven't met'). A National Institute of Dramatic Art (NIDA) graduate, he made his mark with his set for Lindy Hume's 1992 *Carmen* for West Australian Opera.

Right: Designer Dan Potra visits Wardrobe to inspect progress on his costumes for Nabucco.

Stirring the pot

Not surprisingly, he prefers to work with directors who share his enthusiasm for stirring the pot. 'When I collaborate with people like Lindy and David Freeman, our discussions are often—how should I put it—*robust*. We let the ideas clash until the strongest one wins.'

Potra's costumes for *Nabucco* demanded a considerable amount of historical research. By contrast, when Stephen Curtis worked on Simon Phillips' 2005 *La bohème* production, he only had to leave his studio in Sydney's inner west and stroll down the main street to be surrounded by the contemporary equivalents of Puccini's bohemians.

Curtis, who considers opera's collaborative approach to be its biggest attraction, grew up in the country, where he saw almost no theatre but staged elaborate puppet performances for his family (he made the puppets and sets himself). Like Potra he graduated from NIDA, where John Bell saw his designs and asked him to create *The Venetian Twins* for the Sydney Theatre Company.

In contrast to the isolation of his career as a puppeteer, today Curtis spends 'hours and hours' in front of the model box with the director. He's done so many shows with Simon Phillips that their communication has evolved into 'a kind of shorthand'.

He has also collaborated with conductors on his set designs, an approach which he describes as 'enriching for everybody'. When working on *Lulu* with Simon Phillips, early input from former OA music director Simone Young endorsed their idea of a ceiling mirror. She realised that it would bounce the sound out into the auditorium and generally encouraged the use of hard surfaces because it enhanced the vocal sound.

Richard Gill provided Curtis and director Adam Cook with an even clearer creative brief when they were working on their 2005 **Oz**Opera *Carmen* concept. 'You were never actually told what to do, but you were kind of motivated to do it in a particular way', Curtis says, smiling.

Adam Gardnir, who designed the set and costumes for **Oz**Opera's 2005 Melbourne studio production of *The Beggar's Opera,* was similarly inspired by Gill. To him the work

explored many themes—love, honesty, corruption, deceit—yet when he asked the conductor for his take on it, he was given a single line: '*The Beggar's Opera* is about the undoing of one man.' It became the basis on which Gardnir built his design.

Shapes and sizes

Sets for **Oz**Opera's touring productions have to be flexible enough to fit into many small venues, while designing for OA's mainstage productions is no less complex because they have to be mounted in both Sydney's Opera Theatre and the much larger State Theatre at Melbourne's Arts Centre. Sets for Opera Conference productions, staged every eighteen months as a joint initiative with West Australian Opera, the State Opera of South Australia and Opera Queensland, have to fit into the theatres of other capital cities as well.

When Curtis and Phillips were working on their concept for *La bohème,* an Opera Conference production, they set up the model box for Brisbane's Lyric Theatre, where the production premiered. Yet Curtis was determined that his design would fill both the biggest stage on which it was to be performed (the Lyric) and the smallest one (at the Sydney Opera House). His concept thus featured a dilapidated three-storey apartment block that was being renovated from the top down. In Brisbane the third storey was 'vacated for renovations', while in Sydney it could be removed without sacrificing the integrity of the whole.

The discrepancy in size between OA's two main performance venues is a source of considerable angst for the company's technical department. The assumption is that a small set will lose impact in Melbourne, and yet sometimes extra space around it improves a design, says OA's technical production director Chris Potter. By contrast, a set that appears cramped in Sydney can look as bad on the State Theatre's bigger stage. 'You just cannot tell'.

When turning concept into reality—a long and arduous process—designers interact with a range of OA technical personnel, beginning with Potter and technical administration director Chris Yates.

Technical solutions

Yates devotes the bulk of his time to planning, but is ultimately responsible for sets and costumes being ready in time and within budget. He also makes sure the technical side of the show runs smoothly once it has moved into the theatre.

Potter, who enjoys listening to a wide variety of operas and attends all OA's productions,

Left: Designer Stephen Curtis amid costumes for *La bohème*: he took his inspiration from contemporary street fashion.

has a more hands-on role. His love affair with theatre began at the age of 16 when he saw Harry M. Miller's production of *Hair* at the Metro in Sydney's King's Cross. 'At the time it upset everybody—I thought it was fantastic', he recalls. Determined to be part of the theatre world, he approached the Metro for a job. Its stage door manager sent him to town on an errand, and when three errands later the man realised that young Potter had been running all the way to the city and back each time, he offered him a position.

But Potter quickly became bored with nightly *Hair* performances. 'It was very repetitive and after a while it no longer seemed all that wild.' So he switched to opera, where working 'in rep'—changing sets every night—presented a technical challenge. Potter became head mechanist at the Arts Centre before moving into OA's management.

His role is to work out the practical detail of how a production is going to be built. To begin with he sits down with designer and model and tries to visualise the components of the design. 'Because the whole can baffle you before you start.'

It is crucial to gain an early understanding of what the designer expects the set to do. 'A model sitting on a table may look simple, until you realise it has to lift up, turn around and go backwards.'

There are limits to what Workshop can achieve, particularly because OA is a repertory company that needs to change its sets several times a week. Hydraulics, automation and electronic devices, besides being prohibitively expensive, can wreak havoc in such an environment. Hence they are the design elements most likely to elicit a 'No' from Potter.

When set up and left alone, as they are in commercial musicals, these high-tech devices can perform miracles, he explains, but OA's sets have to be pulled apart and reassembled in a hurry. The computer unit from which automation runs can lose its memory when disconnected and re-plugged, and hydraulic hoses can develop air locks in the lines. Fixing such glitches can take an entire day, when stage crew frequently have less than three hours to dismantle one set, assemble the next one and refocus all the lights. 'If a crucial computer unit lost its memory 45 minutes before curtain up, the stage manager would have to apologise to the audience and there'd be no show', Potter says.

Once he has established that Workshop will be able to build a design, the model is presented to the company, and then the Workshop director costs it.

When Hannes Finger retired from OA in 2000 after 35 years with the company, 28 of those as Workshop director, he'd overseen the costing and building of 110 opera sets. In 2005 he was still costing the occasional production.

Finger was born in Germany in 1935 and worked as a cabinetmaker, toolmaker, stage hand and actor before migrating to Australia in 1968. He started working as a props maker

Right: Adam Gardnir discusses his design for *The Beggar's Opera* with Richard Gill.

for one of OA's forerunners, the Elizabethan Theatre Trust Opera Company, where he became head mechanist. A few detours later he was appointed Workshop director at The Australian Opera.

Costing a production involves dissecting the design and working out the amount of steel and timber, the number of hours and the types of craftspeople that building it would require, he says: 'When you get the model, you sit down and study it and sometimes you say to yourself: "This is a shit design—really, I don't like it at all." And then you have to fight back these emotions and say, "But I have to cost it anyway".'

A key relationship

Although an artistic sensibility is essential for the job ('My predecessor never went to see a show—he preferred to stay home and smoke cigars'), a workshop director can only say no for technical reasons. Yet Finger cared so deeply about the aesthetics of design ('Opera is beautiful if you want to know about it') that he would sometimes go upstairs, find the boss and give him a piece of his mind. 'Look Adrian', he'd advise, 'this design is shithouse'. Sometimes, he says, he'd win because he'd point out things of which management might not have been aware.

He found most designers a joy to work with, however. 'I built sets with dozens of them—good designers, clever designers, nice designers, dumb designers—and there were great battles, lovely battles. It's beautiful to put your dagger in a bad opinion.'

Most designers were grateful to hear his advice. 'When they dream up their sets, they *really* like them, but they haven't the slightest clue of how to build them. So you try to help them, but you also try to steer them in the direction you want them to go.'

Finger considered a management directive to trim costs (a frequent occurrence) a golden opportunity for entering into negotiations with a designer. 'I'd tell him or her, "They say it's too expensive. *Ja*, what can we do now?". We'd go over the design and I'd point out the bits I don't like and say, "I think there might be a cheaper way of doing that you know…"'

Duncan Stemler, who was appointed workshop director in 2005 (both Finger's successors moved on after short stints with the company), is a former architect who turned to interior design (he was responsible for the interior of Sydney's Rockpool restaurant) when he discovered that dealing with councils and builders did not appeal to him. He was freelancing as a sculptor (one of his works, *Blow Hole*, is on permanent display in Melbourne's Docklands district) when The Australian Opera asked him to head its technical drawing department. He stayed for a decade, leaving in 2001 to pursue other interests before returning as Workshop director.

Left: Technical administration director Chris Yates and technical production director Chris Potter inspect a set in the loading dock of the Sydney Opera House.

When costing a design, Stemler studies it partly with a view to finding out if building it will keep his staff busy. 'You can't expect a designer to provide you with a blueprint for keeping Workshop gainfully employed, but you can establish which parts of a set can be built quickly to ensure carpenters and welders have work down the line.'

He also factors in the unknown. 'Since you need to thrash out the detail as you go along, you have to be flexible in your estimations.'

The Scenic Art and Props departments do their own cost estimates, and if the overall projection is too high, the design is simplified—a room may not get a ceiling, or the number of windows may be reduced. 'You leave out things in such a way that the audience doesn't realise they were ever there', says Potter.

When cost estimates have been finalised and the budget approved, technical drawing office staff turn the designer's model and sketches into construction drawings.

Right: Props manager David Wilson and Workshop buyer Alex Olup hold court in Workshop.

On the drawing board

Kerryanne Jensen was 15 when she won tickets to *Jesus Christ Superstar* at Sydney's Capitol Theatre. The revolving dome so captivated her that she decided on a career in theatre design. She started with the opera company in 1979, acquiring experience as a props maker, scenic art painter and dresser before leaving to work in TV, film, commercial theatre and theatre consultancy. She returned to OA in 2001, becoming head of Technical Drawing before leaving in 2005.

To draftspeople the designer's 3-D model is the Bible, she says. 'We follow it to the last detail, which means a bad model will look just as bad on stage.' Some designers supplement their 3-D models with comprehensive notes on colour and texture, and the Workshop director clarifies details like the type of materials to be used, whether steel frames have to be ply-clad, where joints should be made and how the physics of the set works.

Jensen sometimes discovers that visual compromises can improve a design technically, but she never makes such changes without consulting the designer.

When the drawings are ready, she distributes them to the steelworkers, carpenters, scenic artists and welders in whose hands they become reality.

Controlling the purse

Workshop keeps track of its expenses from the moment it starts building, thanks to the efforts of its administration coordinator, Janikka Valtilla-Eriksson. A textile artist trained in Sweden, she helped out in the technical department when Hannes Finger was incapacitated for two months in 1996. Her role was to keep staff organised, but she

introduced housekeeping practices that were so popular the company asked her to stay on and expand them.

The most important of these was financial administration. When Valtilla-Eriksson first arrived at OA, Workshop had no system for keeping tabs on expenses. 'Once they'd finished building a set they'd add it all up and have a collective heart attack', she says, with a chuckle. There'd be heated discussions over reams of old-fashioned accounting paper, and Valtilla-Eriksson remembers how one day she sat down and made a few sums on the back on an envelope. 'Here, this is how it is', she told her astonished colleagues. Props manager David Wilson took her scribbles home and came up with a spreadsheet model for recording wardrobe, props and technical costs on a daily basis.

Today Valtilla-Eriksson uses a more sophisticated version of that system. She also monitors progress, makes sure everybody has the information required for dealing with the building process, and keeps the mechanist crew at the Opera House in the loop. If part of a set breaks during the season, she arranges for it to be returned to Workshop, which fixes it before the next performance.

Today's sets are sturdier than those of a few decades ago, and damage is rare, but sets for remounts of old productions—*Tosca* for example, which turned twenty-four in 2005—have to be modified to meet current occupational health and safety standards. 'We used to climb up the back of that old war horse to put bolts in pieces of scenery, and you'd be hanging onto a piece of timber with one hand while you did it', Potter recalls. Today the law demands that mechanists work on platforms with handrails and that a structural engineer signs off on the safety of every set.

Works of art

Head scenic artist Sharna Flowers spends much of her working life on platforms: she creates the surfaces—wooden, textured, marbled—that designers demand and covers them in the paints of their choice.

Each set presents unique scenic challenges. For example, in *Nabucco* Dan Potra wanted a Babylonian wall (not the exploding one) covered in peacock-coloured tiles. Flowers had to find a way to achieve the intense colour he'd envisaged—on the slippery surface of the tiles. She succeeded in that instance, though not when Roger Kirk wanted the floor of his *Manon* design finished in a shiny, glass-like resin. When Flowers pointed out that on an insufficiently ventilated stage, resin's strong odour might cause difficulties for performers, Kirk agreed to settle for a paint that produced the same finish. 'If designers get the impression that you can achieve the look they're after, they relax and the process becomes

Left: Brian Thomson's design for *Madeline Lee* takes shape in Workshop.

collaborative', Flowers says. 'It's when they suspect that you don't know what they're talking about that they stamp their feet.'

Scenery is usually ready for painting around six months after the design presentation. It's a physically demanding job that involves climbing up ladders, carrying buckets and running around, and by the end of the week Flowers, who qualified as a theatre designer in the UK and freelanced there before joining OA in 2003, is often too exhausted to contemplate anything but rest. 'Opera is an all-consuming passion', she says.

Right: Head scenic artist Sharna Flowers paints the bomber in the lead-up to *Madeline Lee*.

Put to the test

Workshop sometimes tests parts of the set on stage as it is being built, in a so-called 'Baupraube', to establish it will perform as designed.

A Baupraube rarely includes props, and even the model seldom displays such fine detail. At the end of the design presentation OA's Props manager David Wilson therefore meets with the designer to establish the production's requirements. Afterwards he makes technical drawings for the craftspeople who build OA's props. He goes to great pains to ensure that staff understand what is expected of them, 'because it's easy for someone to go off on the wrong tangent and by the time it's discovered you could have spent thousands of dollars barking up the wrong tree'.

There was an incident with a horse, for example, where the designer had asked for a 3-D sculpted statue and Wilson, who was looking for ways to cut costs, suggested a two-dimensional version. The designer was overseas but word came back that yes, he had given his consent. Yet when he arrived at the Opera Centre weeks later, he took one look at the horse and said, 'I thought it was going to be 3-D'. The message had never reached him and because he'd been affronted, he dug his heels in.

Designers can be particular, Wilson says, but seeing the finished product on stage often makes one realise it was worth the trouble. In *Lulu,* for example, Stephen Curtis had specified a huge black sofa with panels covered in black leopard print against a silver vinyl background, and a zebra-skin cushioned seat in the centre.

Wilson knew it would be impossible to buy silver vinyl with black leopard spots on it. Instead, he scoured the internet for silver vinyl and when he'd found it, looked for a leopard print design. At this point he discovered that leopards, cheetahs and even tigers have spots, and that they all come in different shapes. When he raised the issue with Curtis, the designer thought he was having him on. 'I want leopard spots, like in my drawing', he told Wilson, who pointed out that Curtis' drawing in fact showed cheetah spots. Curtis was not interested in the finer points, so Wilson ordered a cheetah print

design from the internet. He took it to a screen printer and had it printed in black on the silver vinyl. 'It looked fantastic.'

The sofa itself was built by a craftsman, whom Wilson describes as 'a very rare breed'. Good sculptors are even more difficult to find and OA needed several for the set of *The Love for Three Oranges*. Often they are artists who work for the company as casuals. Supervising them requires a diplomatic approach. 'If you tell a creative person, "Oh look, you're doing that wrong, do it this way", it will get their backs up and you'll get nowhere', Wilson says.

People sometimes ask him why he doesn't just buy props, to which his response is: 'Yeah right, go to the little props shop around the corner and buy that 17th–century menorah.' Antique and second-hand shops are an invaluable source of materials, and he does buy the odd chair from Ikea. And sometimes he'll create a prop by cutting off the bottom of one object and gluing it to the top of another one, then chopping that in half and covering it in fibreglass—theatre is illusion.

Wilson had been working as a telecommunications technician for thirteen years when he made his first visit to the theatre. He subsequently resigned from his job and enrolled for a three-year acting course, working as an actor until a position for a props maker became available at the opera company. He derives great satisfaction from his job, even though he says it consumes his life—he can't rest until he's solved a problem, brings home work almost every night and spends most weekends in the workshop.

Dan Potra may have established a work/family balance, but he still finds things to worry about—the first time he sees his set on stage, for example. 'It can be a frightening experience', he says. 'As the image which was going to be the key to the entire design appears, you suddenly realise that the people sitting at the back can't see it.'

Misjudging sight lines is the most common mistake designers make, and when it happens, Workshop has one of its collective heart attacks. Anxiety is just part of the job, says Yates: 'You're constantly fretting: How are we ever going to build this show on time? How are we going to do this scene change? Will this hydraulic thing work?' He laughs: 'It never stops either—we churn out a different show each night; it just grates along, and you sometimes get to the point where you think, "I don't know whether I'm coming or going!".'

Yet opera gets in your blood. 'I've worked in theatre for twenty-five years and opera is just the best. It has everything—divas, stress, fun. When it all comes together, it's magic.'

Left: Carpenter Sam Richards at work on the bomber's upper deck.

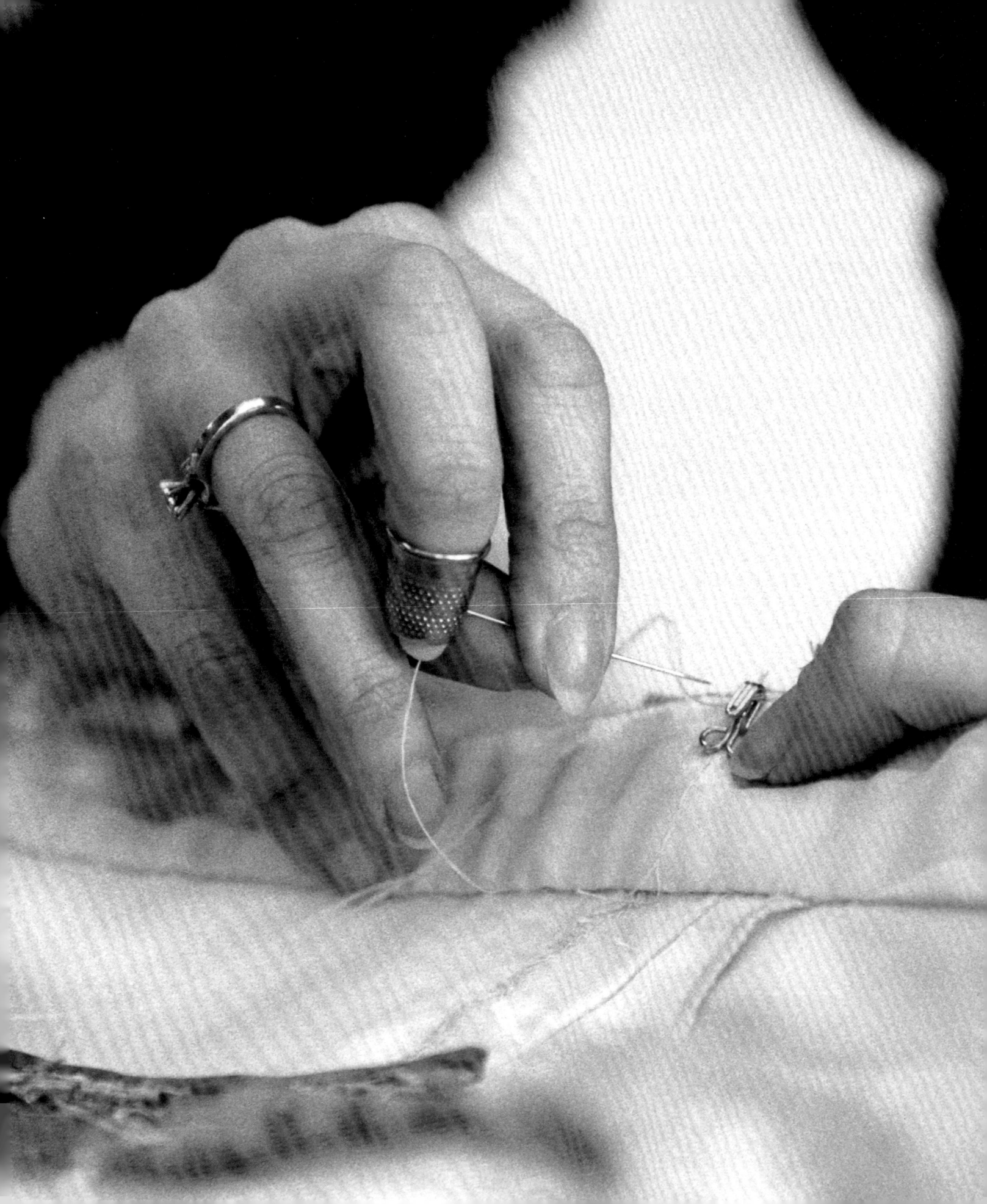

CHAPTER EIGHT

COSTUME DRAMA

To Tony Award-winning costume designer Roger Kirk, the thought of doing a Broadway show conjures up images of taxi interiors. 'When you work in New York you spend hours in traffic', he says. 'You travel from the producer's office to your own office to the people who make the men's costumes to the people who make the women's costumes to the shoe manufacturers, the wig designers, the milliners. Sometimes it feels as if you're living in a taxi.'

In contrast, working at the Opera Centre in Surry Hills is Kirk's idea of going to heaven. 'Very few performing arts companies still have a facility that accommodates Wardrobe, Wigs and Art under one roof', he says. 'It enables the costume designer to become part of the family while working on a production.'

Kirk, whose recent designs for OA include *Manon Lescaut* (1997), *The Gypsy Princess* (2001), *Iolanthe* (2002), *Manon* (2004) and *HMS Pinafore/Trial by Jury* (2005), grew up in Sydney's Rose Bay and started his career as a scenery painter for an amateur theatre company. He joined the Australian Broadcasting Corporation (ABC) as a stage hand and eventually became a designer there, branching out from television to theatre, the film industry and opera.

Like the set designer, the costume designer works in close collaboration with the director. Sometimes it's the same person. For OA's 2004 production of Massenet's *Manon*, for example, Kirk's brief was to create a new set that would incorporate the costumes he'd previously designed for the company's 1997 production of Puccini's *Manon Lescaut*. He also needed to add new ones to fill the gaps, since Massenet's opera is on a much larger scale than Puccini's. The look was to be 1780, the period in which the opera is set. Kirk recreated it by reading widely, studying the period films *Barry Lyndon* and *Les Liaisons Dangereuses* and listening to the music 'again and again and again'.

Left: Deft hands make light work in the Wardrobe department.

For the 2004 double bill, *Baroque Masterworks*, Gabriela Tylesova designed both the set and costumes, aiming for a timeless visual impact rather than a detailed recreation of a specific period. Tylesova, a NIDA graduate whose other credits for OA include *Sweeney Todd* (2001), *L'elisir d'amore* (2001) and *Salome* (2003), began her career as a puppet designer in her native Prague and came to Australia in the 1990s.

Right: Keeping track of accessories.

The concept for Monteverdi's *Il combattimento di Tancredi e Clorinda,* the first opera in the *Baroque Masterworks* double bill, was to draw comparisons between the Christian–Muslim conflict of the Middle Ages and that of the present. In the piece, a Christian knight is infatuated with a Saracen woman but mistakes her for a man and kills her in combat. In staging the piece, director Patrick Nolan solved the dilemma of the principals having to perform music while fighting a duel by splitting the singing and acting components of the roles. While the hero and heroine sang, dancers mimed the duel. This enabled Tylesova to support the historical parallels through her costuming: she dressed the duelling dancers in mediaeval armour (it had to be comfortable enough to move around in) and the singers in 21st–century corporate suits, suggesting that they were looking back through time as the ancient tragedy unfolded.

The companion piece, Purcell's *Dido and Aeneas,* was set in Carthage, the North African port of which Dido was queen. Rather than attempting to recreate the fashions of the ancient city, Tylesova established a timeless look by combining A-line dresses of no particular period with massive tribal necklaces and North African hairstyles.

While set designers' visions can be as bold as the budget allows, costume designers have to consider the feelings of the artists they dress. 'You're putting garments on real people who have their vanities and who might not like the type of clothes you are making them wear', Tylesova says. If you know your subject, you design the costume to suit their figure, Kirk adds. When a production is revived a few years down the line, the designs may have to be adjusted if the principals come in different shapes.

Both Kirk and Tylesova sometimes run their ideas past the singers for whom they are intended, especially if a design has potential to create discomfort—a low neckline or a revealing hemline, for instance. For OA's 2003 *Salome* production, Tylesova approached Lisa Gasteen, who was cast in the title role, to discuss her costume for the dance of the seven veils, which some Salomes have performed naked. They ended up working with Gasteen's legs, 'which are very long and very good', and for which Tylesova designed a red dress with a deep slit. 'It looked very sexy and her husband loved it.'

Balancing the budget

The costume designer interacts with a range of artisans in OA's Wardrobe department, beginning with the Wardrobe director, who costs all designs. For Sue Osmond (she ran OA's Wardrobe and Wigs department while director Lyn Heal was on long service leave in 2004), step one is to break down each costume into its components—boots, trousers, stockings, waistcoat, cap, coat—and estimate the cost of the fabric, labour, trim, pleating and dyeing. She then adds labour expenses (twelve hours for a basic pair of trousers, between sixty and 120 hours for a coat, between eight and ten hours for a hat), combines the figures for each individual outfit and multiplies the total by the number of performers. If the estimated cost is higher than the budget, she negotiates a compromise with the designer.

A former fashion designer, Osmond switched to costumes in her 20s and worked on various productions before spending twelve years as head of NIDA's costume department. Since then she has worked as costume coordinator for the Sydney Olympics and assistant costume supervisor for *The Lion King*.

Left: Seamstresses at work in Wardrobe.

Buying to order

Once the budget has been finalised, the designer's focus shifts to OA's Wardrobe buyer, Miranda Brock, a woman for whom retail is decidedly not therapy. She describes herself as *really* fussy and *quite* particular and she shops to keep Wardrobe's small army of costumiers, costume makers and artists gainfully occupied. Formerly a stylist in the film, TV and fashion industries, she joined OA in 1996. 'I thought it would be a nice little job, buying for the opera. It turned out to be the biggest job I've ever had.'

Brock consults with the designer on the basic materials required for a new production, usually with the help of manufacturers' sample books. Over the years she has learned how to juggle the budget. If a designer falls in love with a silk or linen fabric for a shirt, and the price tag exceeds available funds, she makes up the difference somewhere else.

More often than not she can do this by sourcing fabric from the 'shed' which she's been stocking since her arrival at the company. If she sees a roll of fabric with a wide blue stripe, at $3-a-metre, she buys it because almost every opera requires a striped shirt; if she spots black flannel at a good price, she gets 300 metres since it is bound to be needed for trousers for the chorus in some future production. If a fabric shop is closing down she buys up buttons and zips and overlocking thread, knowing that Wardrobe will devour it before the end of the season.

But the path to opening night is seldom smooth. Brock often has to follow several leads to get what the costume designer wants. In OA's 2005 production of *The Love for Three*

Oranges, for example, Tania Noginova had requested doctors' theatre gowns that looked like the real thing. Brock found that the real thing came in 'funny green and pale blue' when Noginova wanted white, pale grey and aqua. She rang Sydney's St Vincent's Hospital and spoke to the person who handled the starching, who referred her to a laundry in Parramatta.

Above: Designer Gabriela Tylesova.

Right: Costumier John Papadopoulos gives mezzo-soprano Deborah Humble's costume the critical eye during a fitting for *Dido and Aeneas*.

They told her that theatre gowns are manufactured off-shore from a special fabric that is not available in Australia. At this point Brock made an executive decision: finding a substitute was unlikely to ruin Noginova's vision. She bought similar cloth in the colours the designer had requested and found a factory that was able to make up the thirty gowns.

Not all fabrics can be bought. In *HMS Pinafore*, Kirk wanted female chorus members to wear striped petticoats. Brock knew she'd be unable to find the fabric in a catalogue, so she arranged to have it woven. The Art department made a swatch of the colours and the width of the stripes, to which a sample of the required type of fabric was attached. 'It's well worth having fabric made up because you end up getting something fabulous; something you could never buy', she says. She leaves no detail to chance though, having learned that the amount of information supplied (it could relate to anything from colour or design to texture) is directly related to the satisfactoriness of the end result.

Even if you shop for a living, buying shoes for dozens of chorus members can be a nightmare: 'When I heard that they were going to be barefoot in *Baroque Masterworks*, I went, "*Yes!*".' In period operas it is not unusual for each character to need up to four different pairs. Brock gets the sizes and a picture of the design and goes shopping. Sometimes back at Wardrobe an artist will say, 'Ohhh…I don't know about the fit…', and she'll have to take them back.

When unavailable through catalogues or shops, shoes are custom-made. This is an expensive last resort that, as manufacturers need a ten-week lead, demands careful planning.

Hand-knits—for characters like cooks and farmers' wives—require plenty of advance notice too. Brock farms out the work to a knitter she found through the *Yellow Pages*. If a 'knitty' show like *Cunning Little Vixen* is coming up, she makes sure she has the measurements months before opening night.

Brock never takes advantage of any of her suppliers and they know it—if she says she needs something in two weeks, she needs it in two weeks. Sometimes, though, trying to create or buy the components of a costume is more trouble than it's worth. For Michael Campbell and Brian Thomson's *Madeline Lee* (2004) the plan to buy 1940s military uniforms from a disposal shop proved impossible. 'You can't buy those bits and pieces'. Since the opera had a cast of just half a dozen, Brock hired uniforms for them.

Revivals are trickier than new productions because often Brock only finds out what to buy after the fitting, when it turns out that the old costume doesn't fit a new cast member. Since materials required to duplicate an original garment may no longer be available, Brock plans: if she knows a fifteen-year-old production filled with embroidered silk that was in fashion at the time is in the offing, she buys plain silk months in advance and arranges to have it embroidered.

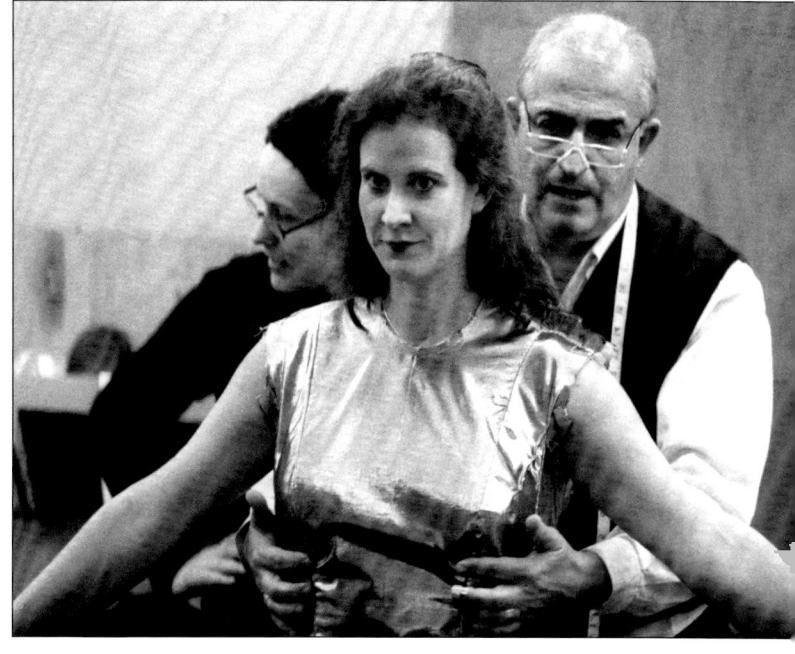

Cutting to size

No one depends on the buyer's shopping excursions more than senior costumiers or 'cutters', John Papadopoulos, Thorsten Ohst and Maruska Blyszczak. They turn the costume designer's two-dimensional drawings into three-dimensional patterns.

Left: Deborah Humble tries out her cape on a walk-around of Wardrobe.

Above: Humble in the hands of Gabriela Tylesova and John Papadopoulos.

Papadopoulos studied fine arts at the *Ecole des Beaux Arts* in Beirut and trained as a couturier in Paris. He had his own fashion house in Beirut before migrating to Australia in 1971. He designed some of this country's first hot pants ('They were a hit!') before joining the opera company in 1977. He only cuts women's costumes.

Thorsten Ohst was second cutter of the Deutsche Staatsoper's four wardrobe departments before he joined OA in 2001. Raised by his grandparents, both tailors (all his teddy bears had fancy outfits), his first days at the famous Berlin company were very tough. 'All the old cutters were critical of me and when I made a mistake it would be discussed very loudly.' He cuts only men's costumes, occasionally turning his hand to so-called 'pants' parts like Cherubino in *Figaro* or Octavian in *Der Rosenkavalier*.

In Melbourne, Ohst and Papadopoulos are assisted by Maruska Blyszczak, formerly principal cutter with the Victoria State Opera. A men's cutter by training (she did a six-year diploma in costume making in her native Poland before migrating to Australia in 1966) these days Blyszczak applies her skills to a wide variety of tasks, including cutting and sewing women's garments. She also helps out when her Sydney colleagues are under pressure.

Costumiers work very closely with designers because theatre costumes have to do more than look good. *HMS Pinafore* costumes, for example, needed slits in the back to enable artists to dance in them. The designer has to bring such detail to the cutters' attention.

Costumes need to suit the singers who wear them, and an overseas designer who does not know local singers depends on OA's costumiers for advice. Papadopoulos is happy to give it, since he believes one of a cutter's most basic responsibilities is to make artists look good. 'A singer who looks gorgeous can concentrate on her role when she goes on stage', he says. He worked as Nicole Kidman's costumier in the film *Moulin Rouge*, and while Kidman might be considered to have a perfect figure compared to many opera singers, he knows how to flatter any shape. 'If your customer is plump you have to make her look good too—why should she have to look like an old bag?'

Thorsten Ohst also cooperates closely with designers. 'Usually they come in here and show you a picture of what they want and you'd say "Excuse me but that's only a front—every costume needs a back!" You need to discuss details like that with designers.'

Above: Irons at the ready.

Right: Melbourne-based costumier, Maruska Blyszczak.

Blyszczak, who has less contact with designers than her Sydney colleagues, relies on her knowledge of structure when putting together ensembles. 'Ballet dancers all come in the same shape but with opera singers you have to adapt', she says.

Cutters are expected to use the same basic design to create costumes that look good on a variety of singers. In OA's 2004 *Norma* production, for example, Papadopoulos adapted the costume design for the sopranos who shared the title role, Elizabeth Connell and Deborah Riedel, to suit the women's dissimilar body shapes. 'You stick to the designer's ideas as much as you can, but your priority is to ensure that the singer looks good', he says.

Eleventh-hour cast changes are the cutters' worst nightmare. Although costumes for covers are routinely made, last-minute understudies who look very different from the ones they had anticipated, are always a possibility. 'We just deal with it', laughs Sue Osmond. 'Some audience members have paid—what, $200? They have the right to expect the same quality every night.'

Maruska Blyszczak says: 'If you panic it's worse. If you take it easy, it happens!'

Even when all goes according to plan, there is pressure. When an international singer is contracted the agent sends over measurements, but these vary from Italy to France to the US. 'So you have to sit and think which one is right and which one is wrong', Papadopoulos says. Cutters sometimes have to finish all but the final details of a costume without having seen the artist. And, of course, sometimes measurements change because the guest singer puts on or loses weight, and the cutter discovers in the fitting that he has to make a completely new costume.

If the job is not without its pressures, the anxiety is seldom caused by singers who regularly appear with the company. 'You establish trust over many years and it turns them into friends', Papadopoulos says. He has made off-stage ensembles for many artists, including Yvonne Kenny's dress for the 2000 Sydney Olympics' closing ceremony.

Sewing up

OA's costume makers or 'stitchers' need little guidance from the costumiers whose patterns they sew together. After twenty years of working with Papadopoulos, Margaret Wright, who joined the company as a seamstress in 1974, has an instinctive grasp of his requirements.

She remembers how nervous she was on her first day with the company. 'I was 19 and very shy and I had to let out this waistband. I'd been taught how to do it at Tech, but my mind had gone blank. Eventually it all came back. I've loved my work from the first day.'

Colleague Sharyn Rhys joined OA in 1999, although she started sewing for the Elizabethan Theatre Trust Opera Company, a forerunner of OA, during school holidays when she was fourteen. Her father and several of her siblings

also worked for the opera company. 'The place has a family atmosphere', she says. 'I feel at home here.'

Wright opted for the theatre because she enjoys 'the challenge of having to think how a costume's parts fit together'. After more than two decades in the industry, she can sew an ensemble together blind-folded.

On the downside, sitting over a sewing machine for many hours each day, sometimes working with layer upon layer of heavy fabric, can take its toll. When the company did *The Merry Widow* in 2004, Wright spent days sewing appliquéd lace on two bodices that were covered in pearls. 'I would go home at night and my hands would ache and ache.'

But seeing her costumes on stage is a buzz that makes the hard work seem like nothing. Once, she happened upon a crowd gathered in front of a music store in Sydney's George Street, to discover that they were looking at a poster of Joan Sutherland in the window. 'She was wearing a beautiful costume and people were pointing at it and when I looked closely I saw that it was one I'd made and it was really just an amazing feeling. I wished I could tell everyone there: "I made that!"'

Rhys also enjoys watching people's reaction to her work. 'When a singer walks out on stage and the audience goes "*Ahhh!*", it feels really good', she says. Another drawcard is the wide variety of creative people who work in Wardrobe. 'When the designer and cutter use unorthodox materials and the Art department paints or shreds them to make something which, when it is on stage, looks authentic, it's just magic.'

Artists-in-residence

OA's Art department creates everything singers may require that is not made of cloth—masks, jewellery, leather work, tiaras and daggers that collapse into their handles when stuck into victims. It also dyes fabric and decorates period shoes.

Department head Samuel Jelinek studied fine arts in Prague and started working for The Australian Opera in 1983. 'I'm one of the few original fossils around here', he says. His personal history is as colourful as the objects he makes for the company's productions. Having landed in hot water for taking part in protests in Czechoslovakia in the late 1970s, he bribed an official to procure travel documents and fled to Italy, where he spent a year in a refugee camp before being able to migrate to Australia as a political refugee.

Above all, he enjoys the variety of his job. In one week he and colleague Ros Keam might work on *Baroque Masterworks,* a historical piece, *Trovatore,* a melodrama set in Spain during the civil war, *Manon*, an 18th-century period piece, and *Madeline Lee*, a contemporary Australian opera. 'That's a lot of variety.'

Like other Wardrobe staff, he requires the costume designer's input when working on new productions. 'You have to consider if you can do it in the time, if the budget is right and if you actually know how to do it.' Sometimes he'd tell the designer: 'You can achieve this look but not within the budget.' Or he'd point out that the material the designer wants is not available in Australia. 'Or it just won't work.'

Breaking down costumes is the biggest part of the Art department's job. As the evening progresses, costumes may have to start looking slightly worn, or dirty, or even ready to fall apart. Don Giovanni for example, enters as a dapper Spanish nobleman and gradually becomes more and more dishevelled. In the end he is all tatters and rags. Wardrobe makes several versions of the same costume and the artist changes into increasingly broken-down versions as the show progresses. Jelinek uses sprays, paints and sandpaper for the purpose, depending on the degree of dirt and damage required. Fabric may also be shredded or burnt and sometimes costumes are spattered with fake blood.

Left: A detail from one of the costumes for *Manon.*

Above: Roger Kirk at a design presentation in the Opera Centre boardroom.

When a fabric's colour is not exactly right, or when the effect of stage lighting requires tone alterations, the Art department dyes it. For instance, in *Baroque Masterworks* the sailors wore 'white' singlets which had been tinted off-white because white cloth turns grey under stage lights. Jelinek coloured them unevenly and incorporated lots of 'sweat' marks to avoid giving away the fact that they'd all been bought at the same Sydney department store. He colours fabric for other reasons too—dark paint sprayed on the sides of costumes, for example, makes singers appear slimmer.

Above: Threads and fasteners take up another corner in Wardrobe.

Right: Seamstress Judith Meschke takes a moment's pause during work on costumes for *Manon*.

Some costumes are works of art, and helping to create them are among Jelinek's most enjoyable challenges. For The Australian Opera's 1992 production of *Maria Stuarda*, designer Jennie Tate asked him to construct a stand-up Renaissance collar for the character of Elizabeth I. The idea was to make her look like a period painting of her historic counterpart. He began with sketches, then made a wire prototype and finally covered it in fabric studded with gold-plated ornaments. The prototype is still hanging on one of the Art studio's walls.

From Jelinek's perspective, violent plot twists are fun. When someone is wounded on stage (a frequent occurrence in opera) Stage Props supplies fake blood that washes off, but when an artist is wearing an elaborate costume that needs to be kept in pristine condition, Jelinek makes a Velcro 'wound' to be attached at the appropriate moment. He also supplies tiny balloons with holes for artists who have to bleed on the stage, which they squeeze when needed.

Some costumes require close cooperation between the Art and Makeup departments. In *Dido and Aeneas* (2004), Kanen Breen's Sorcerer was covered in body paint (body suits crease) to make him look like a slimy lizard. He wore only a pair of knickers, which Jelinek matched to the colours of his body makeup.

Although Art does not make shoes, it decorates custom-made pairs for period pieces. For Roger Kirk's *Manon* Jelinek sprayed shoes with gold and fitted them with buckles. 'Roger likes to get the details right', he says. The Art studio is filled with books on period detail and Jelinek has many more at home.

All jewellery is custom-made. Jelinek sometimes dismantles bought necklaces and

earrings to provide ingredients for more elaborate pieces. He uses donations from members of the public for this purpose too—an earring might become the centre-piece of a necklace, for example. Everything is recycled. 'We have boxes full of old things that we can either fix or process into something different.' The walls of the Art studio are lined with shelves bearing boxes with labels such as 'Broken fans and spare bits', 'Real diamond jewellery' and 'Secret tiaras'.

One box is labelled 'Earplugs'. These are a safety measure required for working with large saws and revolving sandpaper wheels. Safety is crucial to everything Art does—it cannot, for example, supply a necklace or part of an armoured suit that might fall off on stage, or sharp or rusty or unsterilised jewellery.

Although he loves the variety and 'the incredible people' with whom he works, to Jelinek's mind budgets are restrictive and time, too, is sometimes extremely limited.

Wigs with a difference

Time constraints cause periodic anxiety elsewhere in Wardrobe. Head of Wigs, Emma Theobald, who works with a staff of two dressers, two knotters and an apprentice, says in big shows, some of which may require as many as one hundred wigs, she struggles to find trained casuals to help out. 'There are about five of them in Sydney and you can't always get them when you need them.'

Theobald grew up unaware that such things as wig makers existed. It was only when she was training as a makeup artist in 1994 that she heard about a traineeship for a wig maker at the opera company. 'This place was just so interesting—the company does so many different shows and each one needs a different style of wig.'

Commercial wigs might seem an obvious way of dealing with the shortage of trained staff, except that most of them are made of synthetic hair that does not look natural and cannot be styled. Theobald uses only real hair, except for period-style white wigs, for which the coarser yak's hair is more suited.

Commercial wigs also have 'harsh hairlines', often hidden by fringes, while OA's team knots one hair at a time in the front to bleed the hair into the artist's natural hairline.

Theobald works closely with the designer of a new production, to whom she shows

Left: Soprano Elvira Fatykhova in her glamorous ball gown costume, *Manon*.

Above: Another version of the costume representing the ball gown in a 'broken down' state at the end of the opera.

samples from the hair merchant in Germany. For revivals she relies on her library of 'bibles', or files containing notes and photographs of wigs from previous productions. Some shows need five wigs; some, like *Manon,* one hundred. Since Theobald and her staff can restyle existing wigs, they seldom have to make more than five new ones for a new production.

Above: Northern African accessories inspired Gabriela Tylesova's designs for *Dido and Aeneas.* One of her designs is pictured under construction in the Art department.

Right: Soprano Ali McGregor, Deborah Humble and soprano Lisa Harper-Brown wearing the finished pieces in the performance of *Dido and Aeneas.*

Creating a new wig takes about forty hours. Theobald starts by taking head measurements and a head shape mould from the artist. She then traces their hairline and makes a foundation fitted to the artist. The next step is to knot the wig; three to four hairs at a time and closer to the hairline, one hair at a time. Finally it is cut and styled. When the artist is ready to go on stage, a stylist glues the wig to the foundation.

Keeping track

Wardrobe has two coordinators who keep tabs on the dozens of costumes it makes and assembles each day. They source whatever is required to complete an ensemble and make sure it is made on time and in the right size. Each juggles about six productions at a time.

On a typical day, Bronwyn Jones, who joined OA in 2003 after thirty years in theatre, would be working on a new production while simultaneously pulling together a remount. She might also be thinking of a co-production opening in a couple of weeks while organising remakes for a production that's about to go on tour.

Coordinators are in charge of fittings, of which chorus members only have one. 'In *The Love for Three Oranges* we have sixty chorus members on stage', Jones says. 'On days of fittings you'd have a singer every half hour, with people queuing up. You have to be organised and know where your spare sets are, in case a pair of gloves or a hat doesn't fit the chorus member for whom it's intended.' Knowing the faces, body shapes and costumes involved makes the task easier.

In remounts—70% of Wardrobe's work—existing costumes are refitted on new chorus and cast members. The garments are made to be altered, with seam allowances of a few centimetres to permit adjustments, but there are always remakes when the right size and shape for a particular chorus member is not in stock.

After the fitting, each component of an ensemble—jacket, shirt, trousers, tights, coat,

shoes, wig, hat, jewellery, walking stick—is labelled, tied together and dispatched to the Opera House or the Arts Centre. In a production as large as *Manon*, coordinators prepare 180 different costumes in this way.

In a new production they also document every costume detail, so that the original intention is clear when a remount is done. Notes are backed up by photographs and stored in 'costume bibles'.

Back into the box

When a production has finished its run, the costumes are put in storage in a warehouse in Sydney's Blacktown, since keeping them at the Opera Centre would constitute a fire hazard.

Storage supervisor Bonnie Harris, who oversees the process, checks and documents everything before it goes to Blacktown, because missing costume parts cause difficulties for coordinators when the show is brought back. Keeping track of garments is also important because shows from the same period with the same designer might share items, provided the coordinators know where to find them. She does a second check when a production is returned from storage for a revival. Harris managed a costume shop in Melbourne before taking the job at OA and says she loves taking care of the garments in her custody.

In Blacktown, the bulk of the costumes for OA's ninety-odd productions are stored in 140 large crates which protect them from dust and light. Wardrobe realised that such protection was necessary when *Die Meistersinger* was revived after ten years in 2003. At the time costumes were still being stored at the Opera Centre, in dry-cleaning bags which kept out dust. When they were removed from the bags, it was discovered that a decade of exposure to ceiling lights had bleached the fabric, so that everything had to be redyed.

Tail suits and jackets, used in almost every show, are stored at the Opera Centre, in an area the size of an Olympic swimming pool. Each suit has a label sewn into its collar, recording the history of the shows in which it has featured and information about who last

Left: Malleable head blocks on which wigs are shaped and styled.

Above: Head of Manufacturing Wigs, Emma Theobald, threads human hair to create one of the hundred wigs used in *Manon*.

wore it. This knowledge helps coordinators to match suits and chorus members of similar shape and size.

Finishing touches

Right: Bass Conal Coad, wearing his finished wig, relaxes in his dressing room before the final dress rehearsal for *Manon*.

In the run-up to opening night, the costume designer follows the progress of up to 500 outfits making the journey from concept to curtain up even more keenly than the coordinators. When a new production is being staged, he or she would come into the Opera Centre almost every day, fine-tuning during fittings, choosing lace, ribbon and piping with cutters and liaising with the buyer. As Roger Kirk says: 'You choose fabric from a tiny sample but sometimes when it arrives it's ten times brighter than you'd anticipated and you go "*Awww!*".' He once bought fabric because the price was reasonable and he intended to dye it to get the right colour, but the dying process 'sort of killed everything' and he had to start from scratch. In the two months leading up to the 2004 *Manon* opening night, Kirk was at the Opera Centre every day.

Gabriela Tylesova agrees that it's crucial for the designer to be around. 'If there are forty-five chorus members you come to forty-five fittings because if you don't check that things are on track, the production can go in all sorts of unexpected directions.' Sometimes having spent hours choosing a fabric from samples, it would transpire that it was not available. 'You have to be around to make a choice or you might end up with something completely different from what you'd wanted.' She prefers not to know how much time she spends at the Opera Centre in the weeks before opening night. 'I'm scared to work it out because I might discover I am working for a dollar an hour!'

The sense of commitment underscoring Kirk and Tylesova's remarks is echoed by many Wardrobe staff members. As John Papadopoulos puts it: 'I don't come to the Opera Centre to work, like people who go to work in an office. Making costumes for women is my whole life and this place is my home. I feel responsible for it as if it were my own company.'

Sue Osmond finds it a privilege to manage a team with such dedication and professional integrity. 'I work with the best designers in the country, the best artists, the best cutters, the best machinists. We create art, and for many of the people who work here, it is an expression of who they are.'

CHAPTER NINE

GETTING IT TOGETHER

'What am I doing? I don't know what I'm doing…I keep forgetting the words…'

Tenor Rosario La Spina abandons the studio 'stage' on which principals for OA's 2005 Melbourne production of *The Love for Three Oranges* have been rehearsing, and goes to look for his score on a chair behind the piano. Having found it, he sits down and locates the spot from which conductor Richard Gill and rehearsal pianist Stephen Walter started playing a few moments ago. He begins to follow them by counting bars with four fingers of his left hand while tapping the rhythm with his right foot.

'*Dah-dah-dah-dah-dah*!' sings Walter, who is still playing, on behalf of chorus members not called to today's rehearsal, and '*Dee-de-dee-de-dee!*', Gill picks up from him a few bars later, also representing the absent choristers without missing a beat.

By now La Spina has realised why he keeps forgetting his words—there aren't any.

'I'm not singing, I'm laughing', he tells himself, staring intently at the score. He counts out several more bars. 'I'm laughing for two pages.'

The first rehearsal

Assembling the pieces of a new production like *The Love for Three Oranges,* which takes six weeks of rehearsals, is like building a jigsaw. The first day is the corner piece: the conductor informs music staff and principals of the musical interpretation for the piece and the musical parameters for the show are established. It's a time of mutual sizing up and uncomfortable surprises are not uncommon.

A successful conductor moulds fellow musicians into his or her interpretation of the

Left: Countertenor Michael Chance, dancers and actors rehearse a fight scene in *Rinaldo*.

opera yet never disregards their points of view. 'I may have decided on a tempo that is completely different from the pace a particular singer had in mind', says OA music director Richard Hickox. 'But if as conductor you stick to preconceived ideas, you're a fool, because the singer may not be able to sing it that way. I take what singers have to offer; they take what I have to offer and we meet in the middle.'

Hickox forms his interpretation of a work by studying the text and score. Since he has perfect pitch, which enables him to 'hear' the notes he sees on the page, he prefers learning the score by reading it. Familiarising himself with a new opera can take anything from three months to two years, depending on the style—he assimilates contemporary music more easily than Wagner or Mozart, whose work requires years to 'develop'.

Richard Bonynge learns the score by taking it to bed. He sings through every vocal part to ensure that he understands the demands on the various singers. 'I sound like an old crow but it doesn't bother me; the important thing is to see how it all fits together because for an opera conductor, understanding the workings of the human voice is fundamental.'

Above: Dancers in rehearsal for *The Love for Three Oranges*.

Right: Baritone Teddy Tahu Rhodes and mezzo-soprano Deborah Humble try out a dance sequence in the same rehearsal.

All studio rehearsals (and some theatre rehearsals) are accompanied by a repetiteur who plays a piano reduction of the orchestral score. The orchestra—an expensive animal—has three to four rehearsals or 'calls' with the conductor before the production moves into the theatre, but only rehearses with the full cast in the final week before opening night.

Stephen Walter finds the first few days of rehearsals, with their intense focus on the music, extremely stressful. 'As a pianist you have to be at such a pitch of preparation that you're able to jump with the conductor to whatever they're doing', he explains. 'You have to have considered every possible interpretation.'

He describes the rehearsal pianist's task as 'a black hole of a job' which will take whatever time and energy the pianist throws at it and still ask for more. While some repetiteurs are able to 'wing it' (it helps to be a good sight reader), he describes himself— too modestly no doubt—as 'a very little kind of pianist who loves looking at all the black and white dots on the page'. If he hasn't practised every note and considered the score in its entirety before making decisions about what to leave out, he feels 'jittery'.

Once the musical parameters for a show have been established, it is 'put on the floor' and the director takes over. In the first production call, he or she explains the concept of the production to the soloists and choristers who comprise the cast. While it's always important to put everyone in the picture, it's crucial if a director's vision differs markedly from the traditional—Lindy Hume's *Carmen,* for example, or Simon Phillips' *La bohème.*

Building relationships

Production calls last for several weeks. Although the director holds sway at this stage, it is important for the conductor to attend them to allow time to negotiate any differences of opinion.

'You build up a relationship with the director in the rehearsal room, where the music and the drama come together', Richard Hickox says. 'If the conductor flies in at the last minute, everything is set and he has to accept it, or make a nuisance of himself by trying to change things that the ensemble has been rehearsing for weeks. Many conductors do that, but it's no way to make opera.'

Like Moffatt Oxenbould, who would forego the opportunity to engage even big-name maestros if they couldn't be in Sydney for the full rehearsal period, Hickox's policy is that every conductor comes to every rehearsal. Only occasionally is it so important to have a particular person for a particular piece that the company will accept it if they are unable to be available for the full rehearsal period.

Simon Phillips stresses the importance of rehearsal room collaboration between conductor and director: 'You'd say to the conductor, "Look, I think it would be just marvellous if the soprano could swing from the chandelier while singing this aria—do you think it's possible?" And the conductor might go, "Yes, as long as the chandelier is

swinging down, so she could see me just at that point". Or the conductor might say: "This is a dotted note; I'd like to get a particular musical articulation out of the singer," and I'd go, "Well maybe if we played an action on that word, it would assist the musical emphasis of the moment".'

To former OA assistant conductor Simon Hewett (he left for Europe in 2005) the best relationship between conductor and director is 'open and respectful and collaborative'. The interaction he witnessed between Richard Hickox and Francesca Zambello in *Lady Macbeth of Mtsensk* (2002) and *The Love for Three Oranges* (2005), and that between Simone Young and Harry Kupfer in *Otello* (2003) epitomised this. 'They were committed to their ideas but they could still talk to each other about it', he says. Power struggles occur when no time has been allowed for that dialogue to take place, and solutions have to be found at the last minute. Sometimes there is no struggle because everyone knows whose argument will prevail. 'No one says it out loud of course, but whoever is more senior has the last word.'

Up-and-coming Australian conductor Alexander Briger, who is based in the UK but regularly works with OA, cheerfully admits that he doesn't have the clout to insist on changes from a producer: 'I'm too young; I'm still making a name for myself', he says, adding that in today's opera environment even famous conductors hold little sway over star directors like Peter Sellars or Richard Jones.

The bulk of the director's interaction is with the cast, however. 'You have to be a diplomat who can solve conflict and deal with personality clashes', is how Francesca Zambello describes that relationship. 'In opera you work with big personalities, which is a good thing—audiences want to hear music and see people who are larger than life because that's what takes them out of their own lives.'

The assistant director also attends the first production call. It is his or her job to learn the show, so that someone is around to direct it when it is brought back a few years down the line. Local directors like Simon Phillips and Lindy Hume often redirect their own shows, but this is seldom the case with overseas ones. If the original assistant is not around either, the revival director uses the archival video and the original assistant director's score to learn the show.

Left: Chorus members Kent Maddock, Rohan Thatcher and Peter Axford and principals Catherine Carby, Deborah Humble and Teddy Tahu Rhodes rehearse *The Love for Three Oranges*.

Above: Deputy stage manager Katherine Muller and senior stage manager Bianca Esther consult the score during a rehearsal for *Rinaldo*.

OA resident director Cathy Dadd, who mostly directs revivals, stresses the importance of attending the first production call to hear the director's presentation of the concept. She writes everything down; the front page of every assistant director's score she's seen is filled with characterisations. Dadd has revived John Copley's 1986 *Tosca* production several times, including OA's 2005 Opera in the Domain production; she also assisted Simon Phillips on his productions of *Lulu* (2003) and *La bohème* (2005).

Besides offering help of an artistic nature, the assistant director is the guest director's link with the company; someone who understands union rules, the intricacies of artists' schedules and how things work generally.

Working out the schedules that tell singers, instrumentalists, choristers, pianists, choreographers, dancers, Wardrobe staff, coaches and conductors when they have to be where, six days a week (OA averages about ten rehearsals on most week days) is not a job for the faint-hearted. Ruth Thomas, who comes from a background in arts management in the UK, joined the company in 1999 and now spends Thursdays mapping out weekly rehearsal schedules, bearing in mind intricacies such as the fact that principals don't work on the afternoon of a performance, that the chorus has to have a two-hour break between afternoon rehearsals and the evening show, and that there has to be a minimum eleven-hour overnight break before they come back the next morning. Thomas, who suspects the job drove some of her predecessors mad, says the secret is 'to take a deep breath and be methodical'. It also helps to know one's way around spreadsheets.

Above: A rehearsal studio at the Opera Centre.

Right: Professional dancers are hired when needed. Here Danielle Kent and Andrew Frith warm up for *Fledermaus*.

Role play

One of the director's most basic functions is to coax first-class performances from artists. While everyone agrees that an increasingly high standard of acting is expected of opera singers, not everyone is happy about it. 'If you're doing high Gs you can't be expected to do much else', is the opinion of mezzo-soprano Bernadette Cullen, who says the day that voice quality ceases to be paramount is the day opera will die.

Richard Bonynge feels much the same way: 'Obviously if you're doing an opera like *Romeo and Juliet* you can't have a couple of monsters on the stage', he says. 'But musical

casting remains paramount in opera—there's nothing worse than having someone on stage who can't sing the role.'

Repetiteur and composer John Haddock adds that arias are self-reflective pieces not conducive to extensive physical movement anyway. He has seen singers negotiating such immensely difficult music that they have had to hold on to pieces of furniture 'out of sheer terror'. Tenors in particular 'are mostly just happy to get the top notes without fainting'.

Yet to many in the opera world, good acting is crucial to the success of a production. Conductor and repetiteur Andrew Greene says: 'If you're going to rely only on your voice, it had better be extraordinary.' This view is supported by baritone Michael Lewis, to whom singing and acting have been equally important throughout his thirty-year career. Lewis laughs when recalling a rehearsal in which Richard Bonynge ('We've had a good relationship even though I call a spade a bloody spade') yelled at him: 'Don't stand up there and act! Come to the front of the stage and sing!'

Lewis believes opera will only survive as an art from if companies cast people who can act the part, and he laments the fact that Australian singers get so little training in the field. This view is echoed by OA resident director Cathy Dadd who, having studied singing, never expects a singer to do something she would not do herself. Nevertheless she feels that an opera singer who can't act is like a football player who can't run. 'If acting is not your thing, do oratorio, or concerts, but don't do opera', she says. Dadd believes a good actor can pull off the unthinkable, adding that in opera it's often necessary. 'You may well have to convince an audience that you're a fifteen-year-old virgin when you look ninety-seven.' Occasionally someone who looks like Brad Pitt and can sing and act—'Teddy Tahu Rhodes'—does come along. 'When that happens', says Dadd, clutching her hands and glancing heavenwards, 'as a director you go "Thank you baby Jesus"'.

Director David Freeman also considers the acting component of opera crucial, and if time allows he goes to great lengths to get it right. During the rehearsal period for his film version of *Don Giovanni*, he would take the cast to dinner at an Italian restaurant, where for five hours they'd be Don G or Donna Anna or Leporello. At most opera companies though, the director has too small a say in the casting process, and the rehearsal period is too brief, to enable such a process to take place.

Left: Revival director Cathy Dadd summons tenor Dennis O'Neill and soprano Cheryl Barker from opposite ends of the stage during a rehearsal for *Tosca* in the Domain.

Above: Cheryl Barker.

Francesca Zambello, who regularly works for the world's great opera houses, thinks singers generally work hard on their acting, and that American conservatories offer excellent training opportunities. To her, the notion that acting in opera is second-rate is 'almost passé'. She says most singers will try anything if the director presents a unified interpretation. And while she agrees that film, TV, video and DVD have raised the expectations of opera audiences, she feels that it is seldom acknowledged that acting standards have improved across the board. 'Look at an old movie and compare the standard of the acting with what we see on screen today.'

Great expectations

If directors have expectations of singers, the reverse also holds true. Mezzo-soprano Catherine Carby finds it particularly appealing to work with directors who take a subtle approach, such as Neil Armfield: 'He kind of sits back and you think, "Is he directing this piece or what?" Because it seems to happen.' Francesca Zambello is another favourite. 'She'd give singers some ideas, but within those parameters they'd be free to go crazy.' Zambello only pruned performances when they became unruly, or went in the wrong direction. But Carby reserves her highest praise for Lindy Hume, who directed her in *Carmen*. Hume, she says, taught her how to put herself in somebody else's shoes.

Above: Cheryl Barker and Dennis O'Neill get it together, *Tosca*.

Right: Assistant conductor Tom Woods marks up the score of *Carmen* during the dress rehearsal.

Tenor David Hobson says the best directors understand an actor's psychology, which enables them to instil a singer with the confidence to find his or her way through the piece. 'It's the way Baz Luhrmann worked.' A good opera director is also guided by the music: '*Bohème* is like the perfect movie score.'

Soprano Yvonne Kenny finds there's nothing worse than working with a director who asks her to do things that go against her own concept of a character. A good director will find a way to marry a singer's ideas with his or her own. 'It's someone who is not driven by ego; someone who moulds and guides rather than dictates.' Kenny's ideal is Neil Armfield, who directed her in Britten's *The Turn of the Screw*. 'Neil strips away the unessential and looks for the core. He's always saying, "do less, do less, do less".'

Baritone Anthony Warlow expects a director to win him over rather than dictate to him: 'I no longer work with directors who are bullies—it's just not worth it. I need to be caressed, not intimidated.'

Enter the chorus

The spotlight may not be on choristers, but they often have to metamorphose into five different characters in a night, which means they, too, need acting skills.

A clever director uses the first production call to convince the chorus that it is going to be an integral part of a fascinating concept. As chorus member Susan Barber says: 'The worst kind of director is one who doesn't know what to do with us.'

Fellow chorister David Foley loses patience with directors who treat the chorus 'like first-year students who haven't a clue', or who keep changing their minds about what they want. Yet he loved working with Francesca Zambello, even when she altered scenes late in the piece. 'She knew how to fix things that weren't working and her rehearsals were tremendous fun.'

Choristers also adored Harry Kupfer, who directed OA's 2003 production of *Otello*. Kupfer had never worked with the company and asked for a photo album with pictures of all the chorus members to be sent to him in Berlin. By the time he arrived in Sydney he knew them all by sight and name. He also knew exactly what every person was going to be doing at every point in the opera. The chorus responded to his professionalism by giving their absolute best—they perfected the opening scene, for which he had scheduled six calls, in twenty minutes. Kupfer expected 'incredible things', Barber says, like running up and tumbling down a staircase in high-heeled shoes and evening gowns, but thanks to his constant positive feedback, no effort was too great.

Working with forty-eight musicians who all have ideas of their own is not always easy. Foley sympathises with OA chorus master Michael Black, who he is sure, 'must sometimes feel as if he's nanny to forty-eight kids'.

Black, who holds a Masters in Musicology, became chorus master in 2001, having worked as part-time repetiteur with the company before that. He attends to articulation, sound, accuracy, pronunciation, rhythm and conductor's instructions. He also has to

Left: Former assistant chorus master Francis Greep keeps an eye on proceedings during a rehearsal for *Nabucco*.

Above: Luise Napier directs sopranos Rachelle Durkin and Emma Matthews in *Rinaldo*.

be an excellent accompanist and understand vocal technique. 'When you're rehearsing forty-eight trained musicians you turn up for the first call impeccably prepared and you're very clear about the musical instructions you give', he says, smiling. 'I never try to bullshit my way through.' Black says chorus members often challenge him, but he is not threatened by it. If a chorister's suggestion holds merit he will implement it. Ultimately, though, the chorus has to accept his decisions.

Choristers memorise an average opera in eight three-hour music calls (contemporary works demand more rehearsals), and there are another eight production calls with the director. They have basic skills in Italian, French and German and work extensively with the language coaches. Black is proficient in these languages as well as in Russian, but confesses that his Czech is 'hopeless'.

Choristers generally have at least one degree from a musical training institution, plus a fully trained opera voice. About half the members of the chorus have been hired since Black's arrival and in that time only one person has joined without a music or opera degree.

Above: Chorus members James Payne, in the background, and Chloris and Christopher Bath take a moment's break during rehearsal.

Right: Emma Matthews and Michael Chance get up close and personal in a rehearsal of *Rinaldo*.

Yet that was not always the case. Susan Barber, who joined the company in 1990, decided that she wanted to be in the chorus seven years earlier. She got a part-time job as an usherette at the Opera House, which enabled her to see productions, and supplemented this practical exposure by enrolling for singing coaching with a private teacher, Italian lessons through the Workers Education Association and German instruction through the Goethe Institute. By 1990 she was ready for an audition. She 'picked up' four operas in that year before being appointed full-time. The first year, with all the new repertoire it entailed, was tough, but now she seldom has to learn more than one or two new works a year. These days the most difficult part of the job is leaving her husband and teenage son in Sydney when she travels to Melbourne for OA's Autumn and Spring seasons.

David Foley, who joined The Australian Opera in 1984, studied piano and voice privately. His repertoire includes about one hundred operas, but he says learning new works has become more difficult in recent years because opera companies now favour productions in the original language. Foley dreads the day OA brings back *Boris Godunov*, which he learned in English in the 1980s, because he suspects next time it will be performed in Russian.

After a two-year probationary period, chorus members are offered a ten-year contract, but everybody has to re-audition every two years. If there's a problem it is attended to with the help of a teacher. 'Michael Black is very clever, he can work out just from observing rehearsals and performances who needs to do some work', Foley says.

The chorus performs up to six nights a week and twice on Saturdays if there's a matinée. They work on up to five or six different operas at a time—in season it would not be unusual to be performing three while rehearsing another two. The hours can be tough for people with families, and to accommodate them OA offers a job-share arrangement which enables a pair of choristers to share for two years running, then come back full time.

Being a member of OA's chorus is a way of life, says Foley. Extra chorus members who are hired for a specific opera often ask where the post-performance drinks are, 'and they think we're very boring when we tell them we go straight home to be fresh for the morning's rehearsal'.

Nevertheless, it's a sought-after job. When OA recently advertised for two chorus positions, it received over one hundred tapes from hopefuls. Many choristers would originally have aimed for solo careers, Black says. They would have discovered that they were not talented enough, or that they didn't have the determination, or that the breaks didn't come their way. 'But this is such a good job that they don't dwell on it—they're on stage every night performing, without pressure, and a lot of them do covers and small roles.'

Susan Barber, for one, never aspired to stardom. 'For me, being in the chorus is the ultimate', she says. There is great companionship among its members, who also mingle with principals and orchestra and crew members. Foley loves what he does so much he spends his free time listening to the 200-odd operas OA doesn't perform.

Michael Black too sometimes has to pinch himself to make sure his passion really is his job. Some chorus masters use the position as a stepping stone into conducting, but for him it's an end in itself.

Moving parts

Dance sequences, like chorus scenes, add many hours to rehearsal time. Choreographer Elizabeth Hill had worked as a dancer with the West Australian Ballet and a choreographer with the Australian Ballet when Lindy Hume asked her to choreograph OA's 1997 production of *Samson and Delilah*. She has subsequently choreographed the dance sequences in *The Gypsy Princess* (2001), *The Mikado* (2004), *Fledermaus* (2005) and *HMS Pinafore* (2005). She also works as assistant director and is OA company manager.

Although choreographers who work in opera have to fit into the director's concept

Left: Chorus members Elizabeth Ellis and Mary-Ann Fraser rehearse the masked ball scene in *Romeo and Juliet*.

('You're the detail person') while in ballet they take charge, Hill does not find coaching opera singers restrictive: what they may lack in technical skill, they make up for in willingness. 'Singers won't go on stage unless they're comfortable, but they work very hard at perfecting what they're doing', she says. (For complicated, non-singing dance sequences, OA hires professional dancers.)

When working with singers, Hill studies the way individuals move in rehearsals before designing a 'movement vocabulary' that suits each artist's level of competence. The challenge is to find gestures that express the essence of each character without violating the director's concept and without losing sight of each singer's technical ability.

In OA's 2005 *Fledermaus* revival, for example (which Hill choreographed and directed), baritone John Bolton Wood played a lovable, bumbling Irish policeman. Hill had to make him look comic, but comic movement is a skill that, if not mastered, can easily fail to amuse. A four-minute scene with baritone Jonathan Biggins and Bolton Wood, in which the latter had to get dressed and undressed, took thirty hours of rehearsal time—Biggins and Bolton Wood had to practise getting it right, then practise getting it wrong, then find ways to fix it.

Chorus master Michael Black (left) joins Tom Hamilton, Dawn Walsh and Sandra Oldis for a curtain call in *Nabucco*.

By the time complicated comic and not-so-comic interactions have been adequately rehearsed, the end of studio rehearsals is in sight and the cast and chorus are ready to take the show to the next level. The conductor would have started rehearsing with the orchestra, and about a week before opening night soloists, covers, chorus and orchestra assemble for the Sitzprobe or 'seated rehearsal', the last rehearsal before the show moves into the theatre. The Sitzprobe gives the conductor the first opportunity to rehearse the entire cast, the chorus and the orchestra together, without the distraction of lighting, props, costumes and movement.

Making music

Afterwards the orchestra once again takes a backseat while the production moves into the theatre for the so-called 'piano dress rehearsals', or 'piano dresses'. Here the director has the opportunity to make final adjustments with principals and chorus in costume, lighting focused and the conductor in the pit with the pianist. The pacing, planning and emphasis are still the director's: if he or she wants to rehearse a scene six times, six times it will be.

But once the orchestra is in the pit for the 'stage orchestrals' a few days before the final dress rehearsal, the conductor takes charge. He or she will now go through the piece several times, rehearsing the sections on which the orchestra, the chorus or the singers need to spend more time.

Alexander Briger, who has conducted several Janáček operas for OA, says when preparing complex modern works, conductor and cast need to capitalise on every available rehearsal second. Even when they do, mistakes happen. The most common one results from singers' tendency to take their cues from each other rather than from the orchestra or the conductor: the soprano might establish, for example, that she comes in three beats after the baritone, which means if one singer begins in the wrong place 'it's a train smash'.

When it happens Briger mouths *'No, No, No!'* to the next singer, but if they are not looking at him at that moment, or if they are nervous and make a snap decision to go with what they know, he goes from singer to singer, trying to catch their attention and stop the mistake. When he finally manages to get a singer on board, he shows them to wait, and at the right moment throws the cue: *'Bam! Now!'*

Baritones Shannon Foley (left) and John Pringle flank Emma Matthews as they block their moves in *Romeo and Juliet*.

If someone begins singing in the wrong place in *The Cunning Little Vixen* it's not the end of the world because the audience is unlikely to notice. But come in late in *Così* and everyone will know. 'That's what makes Mozart the most difficult of all composers to conduct', laughs Briger, who enjoys such high-adrenalin moments.

Singers have their own expectations of conductors. Yvonne Kenny enjoys working with someone from whom she can learn. Performing *Der Rosenkavalier* in San Francisco with Sir Charles Mackerras was one of the great experiences of her life, and she also relished working with Sir Georg Solti, who had 'incredible knowledge' and knew how to get the best out of singers. The best conductors accept that each singer is unique, she says, and that singers need to express themselves within the overall concept of the music.

Catherine Carby above all expects the conductor to cue her. *Lulu* was frighteningly difficult, she remembers. 'If I started to listen, sometimes I'd begin to wonder whether I was in the right place. And I'd think, the conductor is smiling at me, the prompter's smiling at me, but it doesn't sound right. Maybe I'm a bar late?'

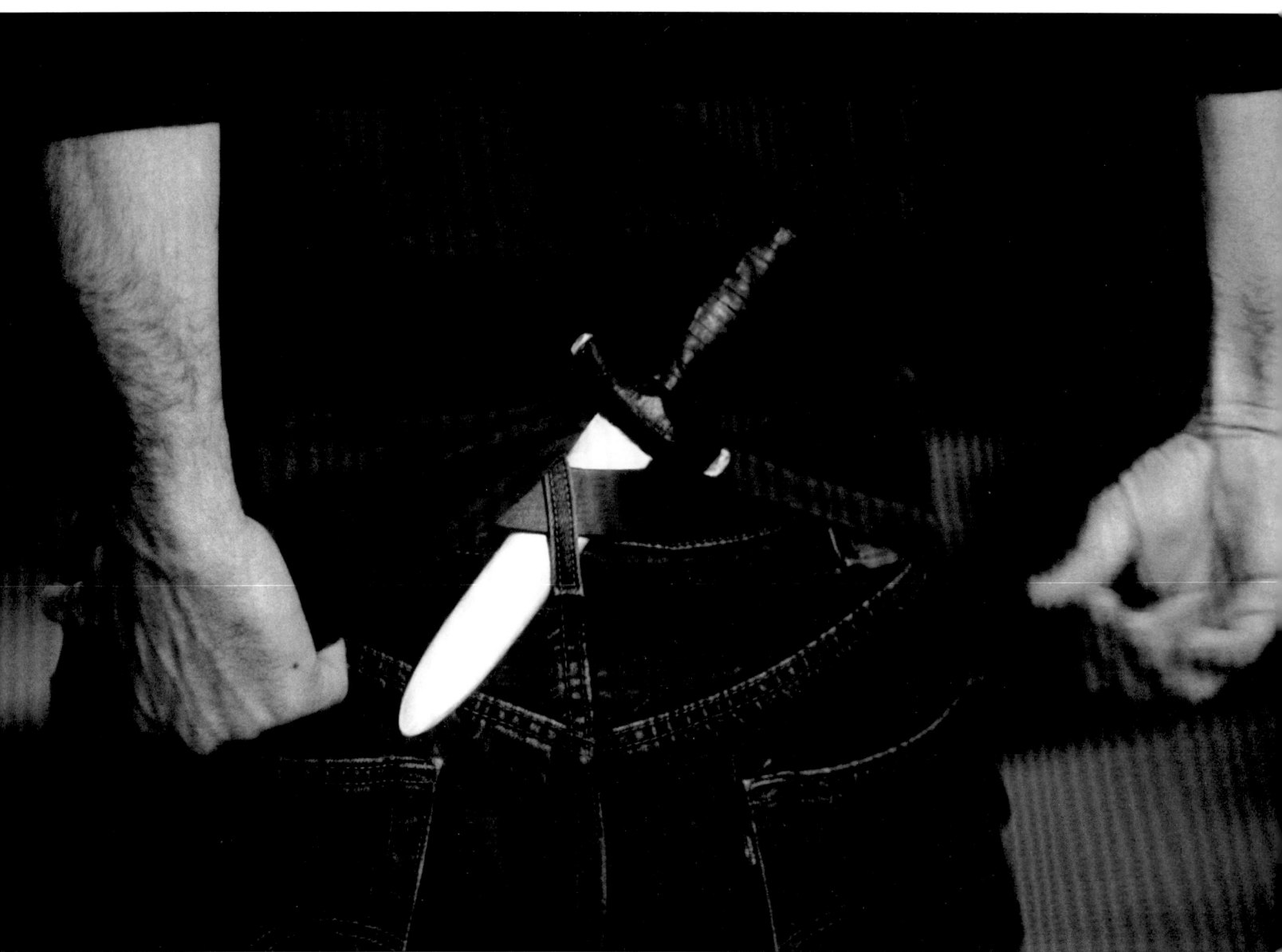

Michael Lewis enjoys contemporary opera but says the conductor's style can complicate these performances. 'Some conductors beat up and down, so that if you look at them in a piece that goes from 4/4 to 3/4 to 6/4 to 2/4, you haven't a clue where you are. David Porcelijn [former chief conductor and artistic director of both the Adelaide and Tasmanian Symphony Orchestras] is fantastic that way—he's like a metronome. He knows how to beat every different time signature; you only need to glance at him to know where you are.'

Choristers also have expectations from conductors. Susan Barber respected Simone Young's total commitment to her vision. 'She'd scream and rant if she didn't get what she wanted, and at rehearsals you could sometimes feel the agitation levels rising', Barber recalls, with a chuckle. 'But in the end she was wondrous—she would spend time explaining and she had a great connection with the orchestra.' Young yelled at her during a *Don Carlo* rehearsal once. 'I wasn't concentrating and sang my phrase too loudly. She looked up and shouted: "Quiet! *You!*" So I never did that again. It was never dull around Simone.'

Clashes among artists—whether they are singers or directors or stage managers or hired extras—can get out of hand. This is why an aspect of Stuart Maunder's job as executive producer is to oversee the entire rehearsal process. 'Part of my job is…to think', he says. 'To be at rehearsals, to troubleshoot, to provide a bit of quality control—directors like having a second pair of eyes; someone whom they can ask: "Do you think it works?"' Yet asked if this means he manages all the directors who work with OA, Maunder makes big eyes. '*Manage* them? Oooo, I wouldn't dare—not some of the directors who come here! But sometimes there's a flair-up and someone has to mediate.'

Moffatt Oxenbould, who seems to have attended every rehearsal scheduled during his fifteen-year tenure of the company, sums up the situation when he says: 'Artists need a reference point.' The conductor, the director and the cast are all professionals, but sometimes a singer or a stage manager, or even a hired extra, would approach him at a rehearsal and confess: 'I don't understand what they want from me—I'm heartbroken; I'm hysterical.' 'When that happens, someone has to be around to follow through.'

At OA today, someone usually is and does, because when the rehearsal period has run its course, the show must go on. No broken heart or hysterical outburst has ever prevented that from happening.

Left: Prop at hand moments before the fight scene in *Romeo and Juliet*.

CHAPTER TEN

PIT STOP

An opera performance is a balancing act between singers and instrumentalists, says Australian Opera and Ballet Orchestra (AOBO) concert master Aubrey Murphy. 'As a musician you're constantly giving and taking, following and accommodating, because singers are human instruments who never repeat a performance in quite the same way.'

Before the first orchestral rehearsal the conductor spends weeks coaching these human instruments, preparing them to fuse their performances with those of the strings, brass, woodwind and percussion. As music director Richard Hickox explains: 'If I'm going to rehearse the orchestra in a way that reflects what the cast is capable of, I need to determine what that is first.' He therefore establishes the tempo of arias and recitatives with individual singers before working on the accompaniment with the orchestra.

Orchestral players, like singers, have high expectations of the musicians who direct them. Innate musicality is all important. As Alexander Briger says, 'Conducting is a gift and if you don't have it, no one will be able to teach it to you.'

Above all, the orchestra wants to see a clear, consistent beat. AOBO violinist Virginia Blunt, who joined the orchestra in 1987 after graduating from the Sydney Conservatorium a couple of years earlier, says the most effective conductors convey what they want through their hands and eyes. She remembers the late Stuart Challender as an outstanding communicator and is equally inspired by Richard Hickox's warmth and ability to draw the best out of the orchestra. 'If something doesn't quite work, Richard will encourage the orchestra to get it right the next time without saying it was wrong', she says.

Murphy finds Hickox's professionalism and tact a joy to work with. 'He's very good at deciphering what needs to be addressed, whether it be a musical or a personnel issue, and he comes to every rehearsal impeccably prepared.'

Left: Patrick Miller conducts Richard Gill's reduction of *Carmen* during an **Oz**Opera performance.

Directing the music

A music director who sets artistic standards and consistently works towards achieving them is crucial to the orchestra because a guest conductor, however good they may be, seldom has the time—or the inclination—to improve overall standards of playing.

Above: Briger's essentials ready to go to work.

Right: Alexander Briger in the conductor's dressing room minutes before taking to the podium for *Così fan tutte*.

Alexander Briger says: 'You improve an orchestra by drilling them—you work on a certain string sound, you tune the winds and get them to listen to each other and you work on the way in which they play together as an ensemble. But you can only do that if you're the music director—you can't change much in two rehearsals and that's not your aim anyway; you're trying to get through the opera and make it sound as good as you can.'

The music director is also the orchestra's main point of contact with the company. AOBO associate principal double bassist Andrew Meisel, who joined the company in 1995, says: 'When Simone Young arrived, she made us feel part of OA. Before that we didn't quite know where we fitted in.' (Young was appointed in 1999. She was the company's first music director after Richard Bonynge, who left The Australian Opera in 1986.)

If Richard Hickox's gracious professionalism proves that conductors don't have to be tyrants to get results, maestros who reduce colleagues to quivering wrecks are still around. It is difficult to throw your weight around, however, when you're conducting friends from your student days who remember the unfortunate result of your second-year Composition assignment. Alexander Briger laughingly refers to this as his 'dilemma': in his home town of Sydney he tends to conduct the same people with whom he has barbecues on weekends.

Briger joined the AOBO as a violinist in 1988 and played many performances for the opera company, with colleagues who are still in the orchestra today. Many were his contemporaries at the Sydney Conservatorium. Now that he is a conductor, attempts to intimidate these people are likely to cause hilarity rather than horror. Briger, who also guest conducts the Sydney Symphony, doesn't even try. Instead, he aims for respect. 'Musicians start mucking around if you don't know your stuff. I never skimp on preparation.'

Based in London, Briger says Australian conductors who wish to develop their art have to spread their wings. 'If you want to break into the big league, you need to gain wide experience and learn languages, which are essential for working in opera.'

Many young conductors start out by assisting senior colleagues. Assistant conductors attend every rehearsal, since they might need to take over performances at short notice. Simon Hewett, now Kapellmeister and assistant to music director Simone Young at the Hamburg State Opera, assisted Richard Hickox in OA's Summer 2005 *Tosca* run. When Hickox came down with an ear infection, he took over the final performances at twenty-four hours' notice. Hewett had attended Hickox's rehearsals, where he took notes, corrected mistakes in the parts and gave notes to singers as required, so he was not coming in completely cold. Yet taking over from another conductor at short notice is like jumping on a moving train: 'You need to make sure you're running at the same speed or it can all end in tears.'

Sometimes the assistant conductor is engaged to conduct two or four performances at the end of a run, when the conductor may have had to leave, and sometimes—especially in long production runs—a new cast and conductor are put on halfway through.

The concertmaster's role

Since an opera conductor has to keep track of many more elements than a symphony conductor, the concertmaster sometimes shoulders part of the responsibility. Aubrey Murphy, educated at the Yehudi Menuhin School in the UK and Indiana University's Opera School (he was principal violin at Covent Garden before joining OA in 2001), says that when the conductor's attention is focused on the stage, the concertmaster needs to ensure that the orchestra maintains the same pace as the singer it is accompanying, and may need to coordinate shifts from recitative to aria to instrumental interlude.

Jo Beaumont, artistic director and co-concertmaster of Orchestra Victoria, which plays for OA when it performs in Melbourne, deals with musical and personality problems in the orchestra, tunes it before a performance and marks up bowings for the string section. Uniform bowing not only looks attractive, but influences the sound that the string section produces. An astute concertmaster, says Beaumont, will know how to change bowings at short notice to support a singer or conductor's interpretation of the music. Unlike the AOBO, which is stretched to the limit by its commitments to OA and

Left: At the start of the dress rehearsal for *Tosca* in the Domain, Richard Hickox checks the sound balance with Stephen Mould and Simon Hewett in the sound booth.

Above: Richard Bonynge and Estella Roche, who assisted with musical preparation, have a final discussion in the pit before the piano dress rehearsal for *Romeo and Juliet*.

the Australian Ballet (individual orchestral members play up to six opera performances a week in season, to the average symphony orchestra's three two-hour concerts), Orchestra Victoria devotes 40% of its performing year to regional and community concerts. As artistic director, Beaumont, who returned to Melbourne in 2000 after twenty years as associate concertmaster at La Scala in Milan (she worked as a physiotherapist before moving to Italy, where she turned her hobby—music—into her career), selects programs, contracts conductors and soloists, rosters casuals and maintains artistic standards.

Above: Soprano Rachelle Durkin rehearses *Rinaldo* with the orchestra.

Right: Trevor Pinnock directs the orchestral rehearsal of *Rinaldo* with Rachelle Durkin and AOBO principal cellist Zoltan Szabo.

Leading an orchestra requires excellent musical credentials, a strong personality and chutzpah. Beaumont proved she had the lot when she auditioned for La Scala in the late 1970s. At the time she and her ex-husband, also a musician, were touring Yugoslavia with a chamber orchestra. The night before the audition they played a concert near the Italian border. When they had finished, the weather had deteriorated and the airports had closed. Determined to make it to the audition, Beaumont hitchhiked to the border, crossed it on foot (the motorist who'd picked her up did not have the documents to enter Italy), and found a place to stay for the night. Having slept a few hours, she boarded a bus to Venice (the airports were still closed) where she caught a train to Milan, arriving at 1 p.m. the next afternoon, in time for the 2 p.m. audition.

Worried that she might miss the train back to Yugoslavia, where the next day she had another concert, Beaumont convinced the panel to let her audition first. She launched into Berg's *Violin Concerto* at such a tempo ('I just wanted to get it over!'), that a few pages into the first section the pianist threw up his hands in despair. One of the members of the adjudicating panel saved the day by waving the repetiteur away, sitting down in front of the piano and playing the orchestral part himself. Beaumont caught the train back to Yugoslavia, arriving at 2 a.m. to find her husband had put a bottle of champagne in the fridge—someone from La Scala had called.

Both Murphy and Beaumont enjoy working in Australia, yet they miss the illustrious houses from which they hail. Beaumont especially misses the conductors with whom she worked at La Scala: Claudio Abbado, Zubin Metha, Lorin Maazel, Georg Solti, Riccardo Muti and Carlos Kleiber. She remembers having tears in her eyes during

Kleiber's final performance of *Tristan und Isolde:* 'I didn't want it to finish, the experience was so incredible. Orchestra members fought over who was going to play in his performances'.

Though she appreciates that financially it's not possible for local arts organisations to bring out high-profile conductors on a regular basis, she misses the learning opportunities that come from consistently working with maestros who keep everybody on their toes because they demand so much.

Murphy, on the other hand, was pleasantly surprised by the amount of interesting new repertoire—*Lady Macbeth of Mtsensk*, *The Love for Three Oranges*, *Lulu*, *Death in Venice*—that he's learned at OA. 'These are major works that opera orchestras don't often have the privilege to play', he says, adding: 'I've learned more new repertoire at OA than I did in my time at Covent Garden.'

But he would like to play in an orchestra that has a strong sense of its own identity: 'If you're part of an opera company, you're always struggling to create that, even if you're a fabulous orchestra like the one at the Met.'

Whispers from the wings

While the concertmaster helps to keep an eye on the orchestra when the conductor's attention is focused on the stage, some operas and circumstances demand the input of a full-time 'conductor's aid' (or perhaps 'singer's aid') to keep stage and pit coordinated. The prompt, whose box at centre stage is partly visible to the audience, cues singers in complex works or under difficult circumstances.

This person, usually a member of OA's music staff, looks after the stage, thus freeing up the conductor to look after the orchestra. OA's head of music Stephen Mould, who has prompted *Lulu*, *Tristan und Isolde*, *Tannhäuser* and

Der Rosenkavalier, explains that the prompt has the score open in front of him or her and gives a visual cue while mouthing the line of text the singer is about to sing, almost as a musical upbeat.

Provided the singers and the conductor are both used to working this way, it can be a great help. In fact, singers who are used to working with prompts (they are part of the German system, in which productions are mounted with minimal rehearsal), tend to be unwilling to perform without one. Someone who has to stand in for another artist at short notice may also need help.

If the company knows a production is going to require a prompt, the set designer has to make provision for the box. This 'hangs' from the roof of the pit, so that the top half of the prompt's body is above the stage floor, in full view of the cast but invisible to the audience.

No two productions are the same, and what may work in one production may be unsuitable for another. *Der Rosenkavalier,* for example, is a long opera with huge amounts of intricate text and complex orchestral and vocal parts that are difficult to coordinate. OA used a prompt in its 2002 Melbourne run of the work, but when the production moved to Sydney, making room for the box in the much smaller Opera House pit would have meant losing orchestral players. The Sydney conductor chose not to compromise on the size of the orchestra, which caused considerable angst among the cast.

Left: AOBO violinist Rachel Westwood readies for the stage before *Tosca* in the Domain.

Above: AOBO concertmaster Aubrey Murphy instructs the strings during rehearsal for Verdi's *Requiem.*

Conductors have diverging views on the practice. Richard Bonynge, who has long experience of conducting with prompts, says in big international houses like the Met and Chicago, where casts are flown in from all over the world and are often changed at the last minute, it's not a bad idea. 'It's marvellous to be able to give your attention to the opera without having to watch every entrance of every singer.'

Richard Hickox on the other hand, dislikes the idea 'on every count'. In Sydney it causes more overcrowding in an already claustrophobic pit, and in general it gets in the way of the conductor's contact with singers: 'Singers often ask me if they can have a prompt, and I'm afraid the answer is "No, you have to learn the part".'

Stephen Mould points out that rehearsal periods are relatively generous at OA and that distance precludes artists from being flown in at the last minute. Limited resources and low levels of funding also restrict the company's ability to perform the Straussian and Wagnerian operas that require singers to memorise hours of philosophical musings in a foreign language. Given all this he feels it is not unreasonable to expect cast members to memorise their roles.

Above: AOBO French horn player Andrew Bain.

Right: AOBO percussionist Stephen Machamer.

Life in the pit

Hickox's point about overcrowding in the Opera House pit is not exaggerated. In fact, cramped pit conditions restrict OA's repertoire choice by dictating the size of the orchestra—the pit can only accommodate 11–12 first and 8–10 second violins, when some big romantic operas typically require 14–16 first and 12–14 second violins to create the depth of string sound required to balance out their double wind sections.

Even when the company performs Mozart or Puccini, the general consensus among orchestral players is that the Opera House pit is a disaster. Double bassist Andrew Meisel identifies it as the single drawback in a career he adores. He explains that where the bass section sits at the back, the low roof prevents sound from escaping, so that players are subjected to a nightly barrage of noise and find it difficult to hear what's going on in the front, or on stage. Many wear earplugs.

Musicians generally dislike earplugs and reserve them for loud works: *Turandot*, for example, has a booming brass section, and *Falstaff* is definitely an earplug-opera. Gabby Waters, AOBO manager until 2005, says while earplugs reduce decibels (members of symphony orchestras also sometimes wear them, so the pit—claustrophobic though it may be—is not solely to blame), they compromise musicians' ability to hear themselves and their fellow artists.

OA uses a sophisticated noise-monitoring program to keep the exposure of players to noise levels in the pit at acceptable levels. Readings are taken for each opera and the results fed into a custom-designed computer program, which establishes each player's exposure to noise for every day of the working year. If the reading exceeds a certain level, players who sit in noisy positions would be rostered less frequently during the season. 'We take it very seriously because noise exposure can cause tinnitus', Waters says. Besides, having to sit through excruciatingly loud performances night after night can wear players down.

Every AOBO member is looking forward to the promised Opera House renovations, which include moving the pit further out beyond the stage. Yet as of 2006 no date has been set for commencing work. 'Probably the year after I retire', is Andrew Meisel's optimistic prediction.

Meisel and Murphy always wanted to play opera, but there are musicians who meander into the art form and then discover that they love it. Orchestra Victoria's Geraldine Evers, for example, learned to play the bass trombone as a teenager and joined the National Training Orchestra when she'd completed her schooling. She auditioned for Orchestra Victoria in 1977 and has been with it ever since. 'In Australia, an opening for a bass trombonist probably comes up once every twenty years', she says.

Violinist John Noble trained as an occupational therapist and freelanced for a variety of ensembles before joining Orchestra Victoria in 1994. He enjoys the opportunity to learn new works (in 2005 he played both *The Love for Three Oranges* and *Nabucco* for the first time), and since the violins rotate between first and second (this applies to the AOBO as well) his professional life is never dull.

While the lifestyle of an orchestral player can be exciting for an unencumbered person, it can be difficult for parents. Virginia Blunt and her husband, trumpeter James Blunt (he's been with the AOBO since 1978) have been married for sixteen years and have two teenagers. When their children were toddlers the couple would spend their Sundays on the phone ringing around for sitters.

In Sydney, orchestral players are rostered on duty for the full run of an opera, since an ensemble that is used to working together gives a better musical performance. A disadvantage of this arrangement is that they cannot see the opera they're performing.

Musicians who are not playing in a particular production have to cover. Depending on the difficulty of the work and if they've performed it before, orchestral covers attend at least one rehearsal and the Sitzprobe.

Left: Andrea Licata conducts Orchestra Victoria in the Sitzprobe for *Nabucco*.

Managing the music

Taking care of logistical issues and generally easing the existence of orchestra members are Orchestra Victoria operations manager Stuart Jones and, until 2005, AOBO manager Gabby Waters. Both come from musical backgrounds: Jones graduated as a violinist from the Queensland Conservatorium before joining Orchestra Victoria's managerial team in 1997, and Waters worked as a bassoonist both locally and internationally before joining OA in 2002.

They are responsible for the day-to-day running of the orchestras: rostering, dealing with leave applications, scheduling covers and ensuring scores are on stands when orchestra members arrive before curtain up.

Other than that, Jones' main responsibility is the allocation of resources, from determining the number of players required for a particular piece of repertoire to hiring the instruments for the Wagner opera that the orchestra will be rehearsing in a month's time. He recalls the time Orchestra Victoria required a rare Holztrompete for a backstage part in a Wagner opera. 'It's quite a peculiar instrument and we couldn't find one anywhere, so the conductor suggested that we hang a beret over the bell of an old trumpet and see how it sounded, and it turned out that it was exactly the sound we were looking for.'

Sydney's Gabby Waters says that making sure everyone is in their seat when the curtain goes up is the most important part of her job. Finding a replacement for a key player—in season—can take all day. When it needs to be done everything else is pushed aside.

For an orchestra manager the fifteen minutes from 7.15 p.m. to 7.30 p.m. is 'torture'. If a player has not turned up and can't be reached, Waters talks to other players in the section, the concertmaster, or if need be, the conductor, to establish if the show can start without the absentee. 'It usually turns out that as long as they're on their way, we'll be fine.'

Above: Maestro Licata takes to the pit of the State Theatre for the dress rehearsal of *Nabucco*.

Right: AOBO double bass associate prinicipal Andrew Meisel.

On most nights everyone turns up, though sometimes they come without their music. In such cases Waters has had to dispatch staff members to fetch scores from home while she digs out orchestral scores (with two bars of everybody's part on each page) and recruits page turners for the absent-minded musicians.

'When you have one hundred people on stage, 1,500 people in the auditorium and the conductor in the pit, you have to solve whatever problem you might have immediately', she says. 'We all thrive on it, but we heave a big sigh of relief when the curtain goes up, and an even bigger one when it comes down.'

Only once in her time with the company did an orchestral crisis force OA to cancel a show. It was the last, sold-out performance of a *Magic Flute* run, and unknown to the company, earlier that day construction workers doing renovations at the Opera House had used a chemical agent to clean a section of the building, not realising that its pungent smell had leaked into the air-conditioning ducts that feed into the pit. When the odour was noticed at 5.15 p.m., Waters alerted senior management at OA and the Opera House.

Everybody went into overdrive and the construction company's general manager rushed to the Opera House to supervise workers personally. They tried everything to get rid of the smell, but to no avail. 'It was nauseating; there was no way the orchestra could breathe it in for three hours', Waters remembers. By the time the decision to cancel the show had been made it was after 7.30 p.m. and the audience was seated.

Fortunately not every aspect of the orchestra manager's job involves crisis management. At the AOBO the job includes orchestral budgeting (a form of crisis management, some would say) and forecasting, which often involves spending hours with Finance costing different string strengths or an extra harp player. When Richard Hickox is away in Europe the manager is also the orchestra's go-between with the company.

Keeping score

Sourcing the scores to put on musicians' stands—both for the AOBO and Orchestra Victoria—is music librarian Peter Alexander's responsibility.

Alexander is one of two trained musicians who administer OA's extensive collection of music (the company keeps scores for the ninety-odd productions in its repertoire, plus reference scores for other operas), librettos (often in a variety of translations), reference books, CDs, archival videos and general odds and ends. The word 'library' is a bit of a misnomer in the context, he says: 'We're a music factory.'

Alexander studied at the Sydney Conservatorium and joined The Australian Opera in 1982. He provides vocal scores, which contain all the singers' parts and a piano reduction of the orchestral score, to singers, music staff and repetiteurs, a conductor's score to the conductor, and orchestral scores for each member of the orchestra. He ensures that everybody has the same rehearsal figures

and bar numbers, so that when the conductor says 'Let's pick it up from letter E', or bar 55, everyone will know where to start.

The library also provides scores to directors, understudies, surtitle operators, sound engineers, stage managers and chorus members. Each score contains a list outlining conductors' cuts and alterations. If there are a lot of changes the library creates a new score which incorporates them.

As far as possible OA buys its scores, especially if they are for repertoire pieces like *The Magic Flute,* which are revived every few years. But if the works are still in copyright (which generally speaking lasts until seventy years after the death of the composer) opera companies have to hire the music from the publisher. The operas of Benjamin Britten for example, who died in 1976, are still in copyright. And while the music for Prokofiev's *The Love for Three Oranges* is not, Tom Stoppard's translation of the libretto is, so that OA needs a licence to perform it.

Using advances in computer technology, OA has begun creating its own scores of works that are no longer in copyright. If an opera company creates its own scores from facsimiles of a composer's manuscripts, it does not have to buy them. Composers' manuscripts, besides being in the public domain, are the most reliable source of the music, since every published edition of a work represents a particular editor's version of the composer's intentions. For OA's 2004 production of *Baroque Masterworks,* Alexander and conductor Richard Gill edited the music from Monteverdi and Purcell's manuscripts and Alexander subsequently created OA's own performing version of the works.

Small, uncomplicated works that don't need too much editing are eminently suitable for this kind of treatment. OA's librarians are in the process of creating the company's own score of *Carmen,* a standard repertoire piece worth having on its database so that it can be edited in exactly the way each conductor wants it.

Keeping tabs on so many notes, symbols, numbers and artists can be stressful, says Alexander, who besides churning out music also deals with singers looking for scores or arias or librettos, conductors in search of different versions of an opera to compare them, and directors looking for different translations of a piece that the company is doing in a foreign language. He never loses sight of his professional *raison d'être* though: 'It gives me special pleasure to know that when I do my job well, the performance is better. Good scores streamline the rehearsal process, so that the players and the conductor have more time to devote to detail and interpretation.'

Left: An AOBO percussionist holds on to his malletts until the time comes to strike.

Opera's rewards

For a conductor, engagements with symphony orchestras allow more time for detail and interpretation than those with opera ensembles. Yet many say there's nothing like the thrill of the theatre.

Simon Hewett, for one, loves working in it because it enables him to develop his skills. 'You need technique and craftsmanship to get through an enormous amount of music in a short time—in opera you don't have three days to rehearse two hours of music.' The challenge for a young conductor is to develop a parallel ability to put a personal stamp on a performance when the opportunity to rehearse a small selection of works in depth presents itself.

Before the advent of the recording industry, which has made it easier for young conductors to build careers with symphonic orchestras, great conductors would spend twenty-odd years working in opera houses before moving into the concert hall and recording studio.

Alexander Briger, who like Hewett sees his future in both disciplines, says opera is more demanding and less glamorous. 'When you conduct a symphony orchestra you get the buzz from being up there with everyone watching you. But in opera people go to see the show and the singers, not the conductor.'

Hidden in the pit or not, orchestral musicians, their managers and their conductors adore what they do. 'You go to opening night and it all comes together—it's magic', says Gabby Waters.

Virginia Blunt finds the hard work pays off every day: 'There are so few opera orchestras and so many people wanting to play in them, that I feel very privileged to have the tenure and lucky to have this career', she says. 'I get to do what I love every day of my life.'

Despite his love-hate relationship with the Opera House pit, Aubrey Murphy cannot imagine life outside it. He loves the melodiousness of operatic repertoire and enjoys working with the colourful characters of the opera world. 'It's sort of…mildly histrionic', he muses. 'Even management is larger than life.'

Jo Beaumont, who has performed a combination of operatic and symphonic repertoire all her life, shares Murphy's love of the drama of the art form, and after more than a decade at OA Andrew Meisel still has difficulty believing that what he does for a living qualifies as a job. 'Most days it feels more like a hobby that's got out of control.'

Meisel loves the excitement and the challenge of following the cast. Great singers (and sometimes not-so-great ones) keep orchestral players on their toes even if they've performed a work one hundred times, he says.

Right: AOBO members Bruce Hellmers, Greg van der Struik, Brett Favell, William Farmer and Matthew Walmsley rehearse Verdi's *Requiem*.

When Alexander Briger, who enjoys working in OA's convivial atmosphere, walks into the company's Surry Hills headquarters for the first day of rehearsals, he feels, frankly, as if he's arrived at the pearly gates. 'You have tea in the little green room and the repetiteurs chat to you and the chorus master smiles and the singers are lovely. There's very little bitchiness at OA.

'And then you come to this building—I mean look at that!' He points at the oblong window of the conductor's dressing room in the Sydney Opera House, where a ferry is sailing past. 'There's no opera house in the world like this one—not in Vienna, not in Berlin, not in London.'

The winding down facilities aren't bad either. After a performance he'll change into jeans and a T-shirt and go for a drink at the Opera Bar, watching ships and boats and ferries sail past, sipping his drink and chatting to other musicians.

Savouring the thought, Briger sits back in his chair, closes his eyes and grins to himself. 'I just love it.'

Left: Richard Hickox talks to AOBO principal cellist Zoltan Szabo during rehearsal of Verdi's *Requiem*.

CHAPTER ELEVEN

TECHNICAL TOUR DE FORCE

Eleventh-hour announcements that a singer has succumbed to winter ailments generally don't faze opera audiences.

If it transpires that the cover's vocal chords are *also* refusing to cooperate, patrons are likely to roll their eyes and curse the flu viruses of the world.

In Australia, not even the news that a last minute stand-in is to sight-read the tenor's role from the wings while the star attraction mimes his moves on stage (as occurred on the opening night of *Der Freischütz* in 2002) will prompt a walk-out: watching the company come up with Plan B is part of the drama.

But there is a limit to what opera lovers will accept. And most draw the line at being asked to go home without having seen the show.

OA knows this only too well. Thus, when during the company's 2005 run of *The Love for Three Oranges,* management was notified at 5 p.m. that the Opera House lift, complete with the first batch of scenery for the 7.30 p.m. performance, was stuck halfway between the loading dock and the stage, artistic administrator Ian McCahon, technical administration director Chris Yates and music director Richard Hickox rushed to Bennelong Point.

Matt Court, OA's head mechanist, remembers that he made the phone call after Opera House technicians had been trying to repair the lift for two hours. By 6 p.m. the company would have to make a decision. If the lift were fixed at the eleventh hour, was management going to hold the curtain? If so, should he call in extra labour?

Left: Checking the lights in the Opera Theatre: OA senior lighting supervisor Simon Tye, far left, SOH lighting supervisors Alisdair Mackellar and Ian Stevens, OA senior lighting supervisor Jonathan Perry and OA head of lighting Colin Alexander.

OA could delay the performance, which was to start at 7.30 p.m., until 8.15 p.m., Ian McCahon remembers. 'Or we could do the performance without the set. There was also a possibility of finding a spot for it later in the week'.

But at 6.10 p.m. the lift started moving. Forty-five minutes later OA's mechanists had built the set. The curtain went up at 7.30 p.m..

The show goes on

Court is responsible for 'putting the show on the stage' and overcoming technical glitches, so that the audience never has to collect a refund or come back on another night. He does his job with the help of a dedicated band of backstage staff. His department consists of seven mechanists, two flymen and thirty-eight crew supplied by the Opera House (they don't all work on the same nights). Together they run the mechanical aspects of the show— sets, motors, launch units, flying elements and special effects. Working in close collaboration with them are the Stores staff (Court supervises transportation of sets), the lighting and surtitle operators and the Stage Props crew.

Above: Sets for *La bohème* arrive at the Opera House.

Right: Props are packed for transportation from OA's Stores to the Opera House.

Overleaf page 172: A prop for *The Love for Three Oranges* awaits transportation from the Opera Centre.

Page 173: Head mechanist Matt Court supervises assembly of the wall for *The Magic Flute* in the loading dock of the Opera House.

Court discusses the best way to assemble a new production with the set designer, then begins by 'choreographing' the movements of the 'trucks' (the parts of the set that run on wheels) during stage rehearsals. Some of them are massive (the trucks for Richard Roberts' *Fledermaus* set weigh about two-and-a-half tonnes each) and when travelling at speed, need three to four metres to stop. 'I spend the first couple of rehearsals yelling at people to get out of the way', he grins. To ease changeovers, trucks stay on wheels throughout a production run. Most of them are so heavy that they won't move; smaller trucks are anchored with manual lock-down brakes.

At Melbourne's State Theatre there is enough space to accommodate scenery for as many as seven operas in the wings, so the crew assembles sets on stage and stores them there. By contrast, at the Opera House sets are built in the large loading dock on the ground floor ('We'll build them on the Harbour Bridge if we have to') and pushed onto a platform lift ten-and-a-half metres wide and nine metres deep. Since they're wheel-bound, they can be pushed on to the stage once upstairs. The space in the wings of the Opera Theatre is so limited, however, that to fit on the stage the set's components must come up from the dock in a specific order.

Assembling a set generates a lot of noise, harmless before the start of a show but unacceptable once the music is playing. Technical administration director Chris Yates remembers the time former OA music director Simone Young stopped the orchestra during a rehearsal to complain about a curtain that had come down loudly and (this apparently added insult to injury) on E flat. 'She didn't expect us to change the pitch; she just didn't want to hear the curtain at all.'

Some sets are more difficult to manoeuvre than others. John Gunther's ten-metre-high *Fidelio* set weighs twenty tonnes and requires special equipment to lift. Brian Thomson's set for The Australian Opera's 1990 *Tristan und Isolde* production used 27,000 litres of water that had to be recycled for each performance. Court remembers a four-and-a-half-foot pool 'sitting in the dock', from which the crew transferred the water.

After a performance in Sydney the mechanists disassemble the set and move it into the downstairs storage area. With OA producing thirteen operas a year at the Opera House, Court has to store as many as seven sets there. It can be a logistical nightmare.

Yet the challenge is what attracts him to the job. Born in New Zealand, he started working in theatre at the age of 14 and became a head flyman before migrating to Australia. He worked for several local theatre companies before joining OA as a mechanist in 1997. He enjoys working in the severely restricted space of the Opera Theatre, which forces mechanists to solve problems. 'Every problem is different—that's the buzz.'

Light work

By the time the set is assembled, lighting technicians would already have marked out the lighting grid on stage and focused the lights according to the designer's

instructions. Once the set is in place they fine-tune.

OA's standard rig has 500 lights, some of which always point in the same direction. But around 350 are refocused at the beginning of a performance, and another forty after interval, according to Colin Alexander, OA's head of lighting who trained in various UK theatres before migrating to Australia and joining the opera company in 1986. A light that points upstage to illuminate a very small area in a matinée of one opera, might need to be refocused for a large down-stage area, in a different colour, for the evening's performance of a different opera.

Lighting technicians work closely with the lighting designer. Nigel Levings, whose designs for OA include *Billy Budd* (1999), *Così fan tutte* (1990), *Don Giovanni* (1991) and *The Cunning Little Vixen* (1997), learned his trade working in London and on Broadway. 'No one said "Put a light here and it will look like this"', he recalls, 'but Broadway especially taught me the meaning of professionalism'.

Levings' starting point is the atmosphere created by the music. He listens to a recording of the opera, noting key and tempo changes in the score to work out what the lighting needs to do from moment to moment. He follows a handful of principles, of which visibility is the most important. Singers have to be able to see the conductor, and when two or more singers are interacting (Carmen and Don José for example) they have to be able to see each other. Safety is a priority too: a singer blinded by lights might miss a step. He avoids sacrificing visibility for the sake of creating evocative stage pictures.

More obviously, lighting has to support the text—it would be ludicrous to depict gathering storm clouds if a performer is singing about a beautiful summer's day. Budget is sacrosanct too. In a repertory company the designer receives a list of standard lighting equipment which comes 'free of charge', but special effects or extra crew have to be negotiated. Repertory companies also have inherent time constraints: Levings' design for the 2005 Melbourne production of *Dirty Dancing* featured over 500 lighting cues, while a typical OA production has one hundred—it would be very difficult to set up more than that between a matinée and an evening performance.

To determine the type of lighting required for visibility, Levings considers the geometry of the theatre and studies the model with the set designer ('I try to understand what he or she is trying to say about the work'). He also considers the designs and colours of the costumes and works out if there are 'issues to resolve, like big hats hiding people's faces'.

He consults with the director and watches him or her put the piece together during studio rehearsals, where he marries his initial ideas with what is happening on the floor. At this point he draws up an installation plan to indicate where the lighting equipment will be placed around the theatre, what colours the lights will be and how they will be controlled.

When the new production moves into the theatre, operators focus the lights according to this blueprint and Levings starts 'painting' his 'light pictures', a process which he refines over several stage rehearsals. Cues for recreating these pictures are recorded on a computerised control system and allocated numbers—Cue 1, Cue 16, Cue 84—which Levings notes in the deputy stage manager's

score. During a performance this person calls out the lighting cues to the operator at the back of the auditorium; the operator presses a button and the light-picture appears, at the exact musical moment when the designer wants the stage atmosphere to change, or a face to be lit up, or the heroine to come into the hero's view.

In a new production Levings repeats the final stage of the process—painting the pictures—in Melbourne (or in Sydney if the production premiered at the State Theatre) to allow for differences between performance venues. Since OA is constantly developing its lighting equipment, he sometimes 'cleans up' old productions—he twice reworked the lighting for Göran Järvefelt's *The Magic Flute*.

Left: The set for Act I of *Fledermaus* is moved during interval prior to installation of Act II.

Above: *Tosca*'s angel takes flight: OA deputy head mechanist John MacKay resets the stage in the Opera Theatre.

Faking it

When the set is in place and the lights have been focused, it's time for props to be assembled. Head of Stage Props Gerard Foley, a former fine arts teacher from Queensland who joined OA in 1992, and his Stage Props crew (two on each side of the stage in a typical production) ensure that the props arrive for each scene, fix them if they break and take them back to the props storage area when they've been used.

Above: **Oz**Opera's set for *Carmen* takes shape at Launceston's Princess Theatre.

Right: Lighting designer Nigel Levings works on a laptop during a rehearsal of *Romeo and Juliet*. He is flanked by assistant director Luise Napier.

For Stage Props crew, an ability to solve problems on the spot is essential. When, for instance, in a 2005 *Don Giovanni* matinée a chorus member accidentally knocked over a table and smashed a couple of plates, Foley immediately ran to an op shop in town to find a replacement. If it had happened during an evening performance he would have glued the pieces together.

Props staff require an eye for detail too. When Foley arrives at the Opera House, the first thing he does is to check the menu. If singers have to eat on stage they need real food to get 'in character', and besides, 'a plastic chook in a setting like Act II of John Copley's *Tosca* would look ridiculous'. For OA's 2005 *Tosca* revival Foley sourced roast chicken from David Jones department store, for Elke Neidhardt's earlier *Tannhäuser* production he bought pretzels from a Paddington bakery.

When sourcing food, he has to take into account any allergies or religious or ethical dietary requirements the singers may have. In OA's 2004 *Rosenkavalier* revival, for instance, Foley catered for a soprano on the Atkins diet.

Unlike theatre food, theatre alcohol is not the real thing. 'We can't have someone slowly getting drunk on stage.' Props is adept at making visual substitutes for various forms of alcohol, although it can be 'a bit hard' to sing after consuming some of these beverages. Foley nevertheless describes his champagne substitute, a mixture of apple juice and soda water, as 'quite refreshing'.

Stage Props has to provide the vessels in which food and beverages are served and, once again, the devil is in the detail. Foley scoured op shops for stemware for Lindy Hume's *Fledermaus* production, since it required champagne glasses in the style popular in New York in the early 1930s.

Documentation has to be in the appropriate language too. Besides making performers feel comfortable, it caters for audience members with opera glasses. 'If somebody is holding

a letter that is supposed to have been written in Italian, yet what is printed is in English and visible downstage, people with binoculars might be offended.'

Flowers, on the other hand, do not always have to be freshly picked. Those that have a purely decorative purpose—the ones in the vases in the parlour of Michael Yeargan's *La traviata* set, for example—can be artificial. If though, like in Neil Armfield's *The Marriage of Figaro,* they are thrown across the stage, only real ones will produce a convincing sound when they hit the floor. Similarly, if there's emphasis on a bouquet—if a principal singer holds it and sings about it, for example—it has to be fresh because if it's fake someone might notice through their opera glasses and 'take offence'.

Stage Props also installs special effects, like the blood drop in director David Freeman and designer Dan Potra's *Nabucco.* In their version of the story, when Nabucco declares himself God, the Almighty responds by emptying out a bucket of blood on him, apparently from heaven. Foley manufactured the blood from a mixture of glycerine, corn syrup and red food dye. Fake blood is available in speciality shops but has a tendency to turn pink under stage lighting. Foley's home-made concoction appears brown in daylight but turns red on stage. The actual drop in *Nabucco* was achieved with the help of a toilet cistern flown in on the flys and emptied out over the megalomaniacal king.

Left: SOH Lighting Supervisor Alisdair Mackellar prepares the rig for an evening performance.

Above: OA's Head of Lighting, Colin Alexander, focuses the lights in the Opera Theatre.

The 'flys', or flying bars, are part of an intricate network of walkways, stairs and bridges that extend high over the stages of the Opera and State Theatres. They enable OA's flymen to move or 'fly' singers, pieces of scenery and sometimes objects—toilet cisterns for example—across the stage.

Foley himself does not chuck flowers when under pressure or hurl blood when offended. He admits the job can be stressful but says he loves the interaction with so many interesting, creative people, adores the music and considers himself lucky to be able to work at the Opera House. The worst part of the job is the long hours: days that start with a morning rehearsal often last from 9 a.m. to 11.30 p.m.. 'It just comes with the territory.'

Speaking the same language

Not so long ago, many audience members would not have known why Nabucco's white suit ends up covered in blood, or the flowers in *Figaro* are thrown to the floor. The fact that we can follow the action, whether it be in German, Czech or Russian, is thanks to surtitles. At OA, the man behind the text above the proscenium arch is English language specialist and assistant director Brian FitzGerald.

When first introduced during The Australian Opera's 1984 Summer season, surtitles were controversial. Although still not universally liked, a company survey early on showed that the vast majority of audience members approved. 'Surtitles opened up a whole new level of understanding', FitzGerald says. The company subsequently decided to surtitle all the operas in its repertoire, including the English ones and English translations of operas like *Jenůfa*.

FitzGerald, a language specialist who had worked in opera as an assistant director, was an obvious candidate for the job. He had 'some German, French and Italian', and when during his interview he confessed that his Italian was rusty, Moffatt Oxenbould responded with: 'It's your English we need.' He was absolutely right, FitzGerald says. 'When translating an opera it takes a while to get the meaning, but the biggest amount of time is taken up by working out how you'll say it in English.'

He created surtitles for eighty operas before leaving the company in 1991 to teach drama at the Sydney Conservatorium of Music. He still modifies surtitles when needed and provides new ones for company premieres.

He does his own translations to make sure he understands every word, and also because existing translations are too verbose for surtitles, which have to be short and snappy to fit into the time allowed by the music. Fast music and wordy operas are the enemies of the surtitle translator. FitzGerald describes Hugo Von Hoffmansthal's libretto for *Der Rosenkavalier* as 'a nightmare, one of the most difficult I've translated'—because the text was so beautiful, it was impossible to decide what to leave out.

In both his first translation and subsequent abbreviated version, FitzGerald tries to retain the tone, humour and characterisation of the original. When Romeo speaks to Mercutio, for example, he adopts a less poetic style from that which he uses when addressing Juliet. Similarly, a translation of the dialogue among the students in *La bohème* requires a different style from that of *Norma*.

Such subtleties are not always appreciated. FitzGerald has had to defend some of his decisions to language purists. 'Puccini's bohemians are not going to say, "To whom were you speaking?" they are more likely to say "Who were you speaking to?"', he explains,

adding: 'I once had a heated discussion with an audience member over "It's me", rather than "It is I".'

He attends studio rehearsals to gain an understanding of the director's interpretation of the work. A particular character might be nastier than he'd envisaged, for example, or the reverse. He also has to know if the story has been updated, because contemporary language is more colloquial than its 19th-century counterpart.

When the translation is complete, FitzGerald assigns a number to each surtitle and marks the points in the score where it has to appear and disappear. OA's surtitle operators, who sit in the roof at the back of the auditorium at the Opera Theatre and at the back of the stalls at the State Theatre, press a button to bring up the surtitle at the appropriate point in the music, and another button removes it. Each show requires two operators—one to make the titles appear and one to check that it is the correct title. 'You could click the same button twice through hesitation or nervousness, and if your eyes were focused on the score you wouldn't realise it.'

FitzGerald's legacy lives on each time an operator pushes a button that makes a line of text appear above the proscenium arch.

He and the stage crew who make blood drop from the sky, fairy queens fly, sets appear and lights shine, never materialise on stage to take their bows when the curtain has come down. But it's thanks to them that it has come down at all.

Some audience members might even have noticed that it was on E flat.

Left: As viewed from the wings: fake blood rains down on Michael Lewis during *Nabucco*.

CHAPTER TWELVE

DRESS REHEARSAL

The final dress rehearsal—or the 'general', as it is known in the industry—brings together months and sometimes years of planning and preparation.

When open to the public, these rehearsals are often full. But sometimes their audience consists of a small number of invited guests, members of the company and media representatives. It offers an opportunity for photographers and television crew to obtain visual material for news and promotional purposes.

At the Sydney Opera House, on a Monday afternoon in late February, last-minute preparations for the open full dress rehearsal of OA's 2005 *Fledermaus* revival are in full swing. With eleven minutes to go to curtain up, the backstage corridors of the House are alive with activity: a principal who has emerged from Makeup scurries to her dressing room and shuts the door behind her; in the communal ladies' dressing room chattering chorus members are putting finishing touches to their makeup and fiddling with their costumes, and outside in the passage a panic-stricken dancer announces to no one in particular that her wig has gone missing.

On stage, behind the sound curtain, the mechanist crew, in black shorts and singlets (*I might not be very bright but I can lift heavy things!* says the inscription on the back of one vest) make last-minute adjustments to the set. Lights have been focused, an electrician is replacing a bulb in a chandelier and senior stage manager Bianca Esther is looking for an unobtrusive spot in which to leave a glass of water for a singer.

The bustle briefly subsides when deputy stage manager Eliska Robenn's voice comes over the intercom: 'Ladies and Gentlemen, this evening's performance of *Fledermaus* will commence in five minutes. Opera Theatre staff and operators, please stand by.'

A tall figure in a blonde wig and a two-piece suit—soprano Miriam Gordon-Stewart,

Left: Makeup chart for mezzo-soprano Sally McHugh who plays First Witch in *Dido and Aeneas*.

tonight's Rosalinde—has arrived in the wings. She hovers about the edge of the stage for a few seconds, then turns and sits down on a sofa a few paces away, staring straight ahead of her.

Above: Soprano Miriam Gordon-Stewart about to take the stage during *Fledermaus*.

Right: Senior stage manager Bianca Esther gives hand cues backstage during *Fledermaus*.

Countdown to curtain up

Preparing artists for curtain up is a complex and time-consuming process that begins around five hours before the house lights go down on the night of a performance.

At mid-afternoon on the day of the *Fledermaus* general rehearsal, OA's Company Office, situated behind the green room at the Opera House, buzzes with activity. Company manager Libby Hill is on the phone to a principal who is waiting for medication for a sore knee to take effect. He says he needs another hour to decide whether he'll be able to perform at 6 p.m..

Hill speaks to him calmly: there is no more time to wait; he has to make a decision. The singer says he'd like to perform but that the sore knee has made him apprehensive about the dance sequence in Act II. 'We can leave out the waltzing scene if we need to', says Hill, who choreographed the dance sequences in *Fledermaus*. The singer rings off, apparently reassured.

Anybody who is sick or injured, or unable to make a call, a costume fitting or a coaching session, calls Company Office, OA's nerve centre, from where information is disseminated and covers put in place. On the day of a performance, all artists have to sign on and if they don't, Hill and two colleagues start chasing them.

In a crisis, these women sometimes follow instinct rather than protocol. During a recent *Marriage of Figaro* run, for example, a very unwell Suzanna arrived for a 7.30 p.m. performance at 6.45 p.m., white as a sheet. Hill's colleague Saskia Howard rang the artistic administrator (management is informed of crises in a specific order), who advised her to give the situation five minutes, but she rang the cover straightaway. The latter got in her car, drove across the bridge from Mosman, reported at Wigs and Makeup at 7.15 p.m. and

walked on stage at 7.35 p.m.. 'Sometimes you have to act first and think later', says Hill.

In another part of the Opera House, at Performing Wigs and Makeup, singers are being transformed into characters. OA employs two full-time hairdressers/makeup artists and hires extras for big shows. On busy nights it is not unusual for six stylists to work on 140 wigs.

Chorus master Michael Black awaits his moment to ring the door bell in Act I of *Fledermaus*.

Professional makeover

Head of Performing Wigs and Makeup David Jennings trained as a hairdresser and worked in salons (he subscribed to the opera even then) before moving to the ABC and, in 1989, the opera company. He loves the adrenalin rush and the beautiful singing.

Principals used to do their own makeup, until advanced lighting demanded a more professional approach. Chorus members still do their own faces (in a new production Jennings would give a demonstration and hand out notes and sketches), but they get help with wigs.

Jennings discusses the overall look of a new production with the costume designer. Some have very specific requirements while others just want artists to look good. The shape of singers' faces dictates his approach unless the storyline demands a particular appearance. If someone has to look very old, for example, he would make eyes smaller and more saggy, draw in jowls and highlight wrinkles. Otherwise he highlights positive features like large eyes and ties individual appearances into the overall look of the production. In revivals that require a specific appearance (such as *The Mikado*), he follows his predecessors' instructions.

Once an artist's 'face' is in place, the wig goes on. Fitting it is easy, says Jennings, keeping it on is a different matter. 'Wigs sometimes fall off during rehearsals, when you find out the dancer has to do cartwheels', he laughs. In operettas, which contain spoken dialogue, wigs come with microphones.

A wig usually has to be redressed several times during a performance, and not always in ideal circumstances. In *The Merry Widow* Jennings would help to take off the widow's shoes and change her jewellery while a dresser would button her into her next outfit. He would then touch up her makeup and redress her hair, all in the wings and in less than one hundred seconds.

Dress circle

Bobby McKenzie, head of Performing Wardrobe, shares the responsibility for getting singers on stage in character and on time. His department consists of twelve dressers (men dress men and women dress women), a wardrobe mistress, Irish Allen, to take care of women's costumes (McKenzie looks after the men's himself), and a maintenance person who washes, steams and irons garments after every rehearsal and performance.

When costumes have been delivered to the theatre, McKenzie and Allen unpack them and brief dressers on each change. Each costume is labelled with the performer's name and dressing room. On the day of a performance they start preparing mid-afternoon, hanging the costumes on racks and delivering them to the right place. Principals have their own dressing rooms while chorus members share a large room which holds twenty-four.

Costumes often need last-minute attention—a seam may give or a zipper become stuck and it is not unusual for McKenzie and Allen to sew singers into their costumes at the eleventh hour.

Though unfazed by such calamities, McKenzie admits to being spooked by frenzied changes in the wings, especially when the entire chorus has to get out of one and into another costume in the narrow walkway (it's less than two metres wide) on the edges of the Opera Theatre. 'It gets mad, crazy', he laughs.

Period costumes and quick changes are the stuff of McKenzie's nightmares. In *Così fan tutte,* for example, when the two male principals swap back to their original identities in the final scene, they come off the stage, turn around and go straight back up the steps, as different people. Performing Wardrobe has seconds to change the singers' shoes, tights, pants, shirts, undercoats, overcoats, cravats, rings and hats.

When an artist falls ill during a performance it also causes anxiety, since the understudy may not even be in the building. 'You can't fix up a cover's costume until they've put it on', McKenzie explains. 'This type of scenario sends everyone into a panic.'

Tenor Angus Wood laces his shoes in the wings during *Fledermaus* while dresser Hamish Peters holds his jacket at the ready.

McKenzie did a sewing course after school and worked as a dresser for BBC TV before being offered a similar job at the opera company in Sydney. He's been head of Performing Wardrobe since 1992 and loves every minute of it, including the moments of panic.

Dresser Sheila Beames would not want to do anything else either. 'It's a joy to be able to hold a coat for someone while people are performing this divine music', she says.

Even as a teenager Beames dreamed of working in theatre. She began in radio before moving on to arranging itineraries for ABC visiting concert artists and finally dressing principals at the opera company. Half the job is anticipating what artists require, she says. (In Miriam Gordon-Stewart's dressing room, where we're talking, a pot of steaming tea covered by a cozy is waiting in the corner of the dressing table.) Artists derive comfort from working with a dresser who knows how they like things done. 'One singer will put her left hand in a sleeve first, or put her shoes on first, while another will leave the shoes for last. You get to know these things.'

Above: Dresser Helen Towers and soprano Tiffany Speight watch proceedings from the wings during *HMS Pinafore*.

Right: Deputy stage manager Eliska Robenn monitors the action from cue corner.

Professionalism and tact are other requirements of the job. 'People walk in and out of this room and sometimes you try to leave but you can't, so you become invisible—you don't hear it, you don't comment on it and you certainly don't repeat it.' And sometimes, she says, you just have to drop everything and go.

Beames refrains from telling singers her life story. 'Over in the wig room they talk to each other and to David Jennings, but once they come to their dressing room they've begun to focus and they don't want chat, chat, chat.'

During hectic changes the onus to remain calm rests on the dresser, and when a change is 'very tricksey' (even underwear sometimes has to be changed in the wings), Beames practises it with the singer beforehand.

Running the show

While dressers support, aid and reassure the artists with whom they work (besides getting them in and out of their costumes), stage managers nurture the entire performing company. Ask senior stage manager Bianca Esther for a job description and she rattles off an instant reply: 'I'm a nursemaid, a clairvoyant, a psychiatrist, a child minder, a gofer and a linguist—among other things.'

The stage manager enables the director and conductor to realise their vision. 'It's always about others' needs', Esther says, adding with a laugh: 'Which sort of explains why most stage managers are women.'

She finds it easy to nurture singers, whom she describes as 'generally the most professional and appreciative of people', and even children are not difficult to accommodate. On stage they are the chorus master's responsibility, and stage management hands them over to their chaperones as soon as they come off. Children who perform with OA generally appreciate that being in one of the company's productions is an honour. 'They don't play up, although of course you get the occasional ratbag, or someone who's had too much red food colouring.'

Most of the repertoire requires three stage managers, one on each side of the stage and one in cue corner. Big decisions—whether an unreliable piece of scenery is to be left in the wings, or if interval is to be held by half an hour because something's not working— are Esther's responsibility.

When all is going smoothly, she and an assistant stage manager work on opposite sides of the stage, ensuring that artists have the correct props before going on and giving them entrance cues. Some of the older singers no longer need them, but younger ones rely on signals. When singers come off stage, a manager will be waiting in the wings with a torch to help their eyes adjust from the bright lights of the stage to the darkness beyond.

Left: Deputy stage manager Bebe Southby and stage manager Crissie Higgins check the score during a rehearsal of *Nabucco*. Director David Freeman looks on.

Right: Mezzo-soprano Catherine Carby hovers in the wings, about to take the stage in *Nabucco*.

Stage calls

The responsibility for calling artists and crew members to the stage in time rests with the deputy stage manager. This person lives in cue corner, downstage behind the proscenium (from the audience's vantage point, in the right front corner of the stage, behind the wall), before a communication console. Today it is Eliska Robenn. She calls every artist, dresser, crew member and orchestral player to the stage. 'It's the heart of it, really', Esther says.

Robenn works from a special score with cues written in the blank pages between each page of music. If a singer has to go up a staircase and open a window, it will be noted over the exact note or chord on which it is to take place. The conductor is projected on a monitor in front of her, the stage on another one, and on a third, the lighting cues. She follows the three screens as well as the score.

OA's eight full-time stage managers are all deft score readers. 'It's essential in opera—entrances are based on single quarter notes', Esther says. Giving a word cue in an English opera may be easy, but in works like the Czech *Jenůfa* or the Russian *Eugene Onegin*, 'it all sounds like gobbledygook' and stage managers hold on to the dots on the page for dear life.

Normally Esther and her colleagues start familiarising themselves with the music a few months before rehearsals begin, but some operas require special attention. It took six months to learn the score for *Lulu*, for example, and

Left: Senior Performance Wigs/Makeup supervisor, Andrew Keshan, dresses Angus Wood's hair ahead of the dress rehearsal for *Il combattimento di Tancredi e Clorinda*.

Right: Head of Performing Wigs and Makeup, David Jennings, applies body paint to tenor Kanen Breen during the dress rehearsal for *Dido and Aeneas*.

even then stage management needed the assistance of a member of music staff during performances. 'When we saw that even *he* frequently got lost, we didn't feel quite so bad!' Esther laughs.

Two or three weeks before rehearsals begin she checks which costume parts and set components will be needed in the rehearsal studio and marks out the studio floor with coloured tape, to denote where each part of the set is to go.

Once the production has moved into the theatre, stage managers are on the prowl for potential crises. 'If you hear someone on headsets going *Oops!* a couple of metres away, you go over and ask: "What's *Oops?*"'

When things go wrong they generally have to be dealt with immediately. If a glass is smashed on stage, Esther would grab the closest actor, give him a dust pan and brush and create a scenario of why he should be in that scene. 'Because you really need the glass picked up.'

Ensuring that nobody gets hurt is fundamental to the job. 'A theatre is a hideously dangerous environment because it's full of people surrounded by heavy, moving things. It's terrifying when people fall down on the stage, or if they don't see a step and twist an ankle. We prevent accidents by being diligent and careful and consistent, and by rehearsing.'

Esther studied stage management at the University of Western Australia and chose to work in opera because she loves classical music and enjoys 'the challenge and the sheer volume' of the medium. She says stage managers are burnt out by thirty-five—it's emotionally draining and physically demanding to be the one on whom everyone depends. 'Once we get on stage we have a support crew of between thirty and sixty people, but in the weeks leading up to it, three stage managers are lifting and carrying all scenery in the rehearsal studio, besides helping with costumes and handing props to singers. For a stage manager, physical fitness is almost as important as the ability to read a score.'

Some move into management, some become directors and some go away and study horticulture. If it weren't for physical exhaustion, Esther says she'd stay forever. 'I earn a living listening to extraordinary singers making extraordinary music, in this breathtaking building. Other people pay over $200 for the best seat in the House; I get mine free of charge, night after night.'

Left: Sally McHugh touches up her lipstick under the watchful eye of makeup artist Fiona Cooper-Hamilton before going on stage in *Dido and Aeneas*.

Above: Andrew Keshan applies the finishing touches to Angus Wood's wig.

As the last notes of *Fledermaus* Act I die away on the stage, she excuses herself and noiselessly moves towards cue corner. The crew, who have crept into the wings as quietly as commando troopers, join the audience in applauding the cast, but as the stage lights dim and Esther signals for the first, then the second, sound curtain to come down, silence falls over the backstage area.

Moments later, when the working lights flicker on, pandemonium breaks out: there's talking, shouting, shuffling and pushing, followed by screeching and rattling as the front room of the Eisensteins' New York apartment starts moving in the direction of the lift.

In the foyer the audience is probably having champagne.

Backstage at the Opera House, it's showtime.

Left: Working in the wings, David Jennings adjusts baritone Michael Lewis' headpiece moments before he goes on stage in *Nabucco*.

Above: Chorus member Juan Jackson's makeup is touched up backstage by Alison Kidd.

CHAPTER THIRTEEN

THE MORNING AFTER

'Die!' yelled soprano Cheryl Barker. 'Your soul be dammed for your sins! Die!'

The man to whom she was recommending these violent measures—and to prove she meant business she threw in a couple of lethal stabs—was her husband of over two decades, Peter Coleman-Wright. The occasion was the 2005 Sydney Domain performance of *Tosca,* in which Coleman-Wright sang the role of Scarpia to Barker's Tosca.

He was far from dead though. Having dropped to the floor, 'Scarpia' had become uncomfortably aware that his hands appeared to be moving, and it took a few seconds to register that the movement was not coming from his body but from hundreds of insects crawling underneath it.

'Your first impulse is to scream and jump up', the singer recalls, weeks later, in the chic lounge of the inner-Sydney home he shares with Barker and their young son, Gabriel. But running off the stage would have destroyed the drama of the moment. So he got comfortable on the floor, with the creepy-crawlies. At this level of artistry, professionalism prevails—on stage at least.

Behind closed doors

But what happens after 'Scarpia' and 'Tosca' have taken their bows, removed their makeup and caught a taxi home?

Watching Coleman-Wright accompany his wife and son on the grand piano in the corner of the lounge as they sing *Pussycat, Pussycat, where have you been?* (the performance is briefly interrupted when a cat called Cute jumps on a nearby cabinet

Left: Soprano Cheryl Barker and baritone Peter Coleman-Wright rehearse *Tosca* in the Domain.

and knocks over a photograph of Barker and the late Princess of Wales), it's difficult to picture Puccini's adversaries arriving home in character, slamming doors and stomping up staircases.

Coleman-Wright chuckles at the notion. 'We've done so many shows together that we no longer take it personally', he says, closing the piano. Performances are frequently followed by functions or drinks with friends anyway, which leaves little time for post mortems. On nights when the singers do go straight home, the routine is pretty mundane: a piece of toast, a shower, pyjamas, a little TV, bed.

If unwinding together tends to be painless, the countdown to a performance can be the opposite, as baritone Michael Lewis and soprano Nicole Youl have discovered.

In a company-rented apartment behind the Arts Centre in Melbourne, where the couple are gearing up for the premier of OA's new production of *Nabucco* (Lewis sings the title role), he affirms that success does not temper nerves—on the contrary, before major performances he more than ever feels 'like a bomb waiting to go off'. Youl has a simple strategy for coping with her husband's nerves: she keeps out of his way. In the seven years they've been together they've never had an argument, but should it happen, she suspects it will be impressive. 'Michael's such a diva', she laughs. Youl does not suffer from stage fright herself, yet Lewis frets over her opening nights too, fussing and bringing tea and generally behaving like a loving companion.

The joy of mutual support is a recurrent theme among people who share a career in opera—Lewis and Youl fly all over the country to attend each other's rehearsals and performances and their biggest buzz is to be in the same show, like when they did *Il trovatore* together in Perth in 2002. 'We're very much in love', says the baritone, who describes his relationship with Youl as the most important of his life, a sentiment she shares.

When soprano Emma Matthews goes on stage her equanimity is bolstered by the knowledge that her husband Stephen, a former chorus member and now a mechanist with OA, is in the wings watching out for her. (She jokes that when they first started dating she was warned that as a soloist she was 'ruining her reputation' by seeing someone from the chorus.)

In the informal outdoor entertainment area of the couple's Sydney home, Stephen, who is minding toddler Jack and baby Brendan while his wife boils the kettle for tea, remembers the 2003 opening night of *Lulu* in Melbourne as one of the most nerve-wracking of his life. 'I was watching Emma from the wings, thinking: "*When did she learn that?*"' She rarely practises, he maintains, a charge which Matthews cheerfully corroborates, although she stresses that the run-up to *Lulu* was a particularly difficult time: she was suffering from post-natal depression and like any new mother, found herself exhausted and preoccupied.

As *Lulu* loomed larger, the couple rented a house in the country so that Matthews could lock herself in a room and cram. When they arrived, however, she discovered that she'd forgotten to bring her keyboard. Stephen bought one from a nearby toyshop. She then found that it took a week to memorise eight pages, normally enough time to master an entire role. 'It was very scary', she remembers, 'and to make matters worse colleagues kept reminding me, "This could ruin your career; this could be the last thing you do"'.

Stephen never doubted that his wife would pull through. 'It was just a difficult time, with Jack being brand-new and people pulling out of even minor roles because the music was so difficult.'

Besides the challenge of some of the most fiendishly complex music in the repertoire, *Lulu* confronts its female principal with three hours of virtual emotional abuse: she is murdered—which is not that uncommon in opera—after one of the most explicit sexual acts in the soprano repertoire. (Lulu's comments on the proceedings culminate on a high F.)

After that, going home to feed the baby requires a little mental re-adjustment.

Cheryl Barker and Peter Coleman-Wright at home in Sydney with their son Gabriel.

Little time for lullabies

Combining babies with an opera career is fraught with difficulty. Bass Richard Alexander and soprano Lisa Russell used to enjoy appearing in the same productions but since the arrival of baby Chloe, they have been avoiding it so that one of them is at home to look after her.

Having a child has made her forget herself, Russell says, rocking Chloe in a hammock tied between two trees in the family's perfectly tended, postage-stamp garden in inner Sydney. 'I used to refuse to talk on performance days, but when you have a child you can no longer afford to be precious.' For Alexander, parenthood has brought more focus; suddenly he has to fit the same amount of work into a much smaller part of the day. He recalls when he and Russell would do their grocery shopping at midnight, after a show. Those days are over now.

Unlike Russell, some opera parents do manage to avoid talking before a performance—in fact there are singers who shun speech for as long as two days before curtain up. Coleman-Wright and Barker try to 'keep *stum*' on the day of a performance ('We have a wonderful nanny', Barker explains), but otherwise they're hands-on parents: 'We always wanted children; Gabriel was a long time coming and when he finally did arrive we were just over the moon.'

If singers' offspring have to deal with periods of parental silence, they quickly learn to assert themselves in difficult situations. When at the tender age of eight months, young Gabriel was taken (kicking and screaming, it would appear) to hear his mother sing *Madama Butterfly*, he let his feelings about her performance be known during her first aria. 'Aaaaggghhhh!!!!' he yelled. He and his father had to leave the House.

Gabriel has since acquired more appreciation for the art form—in Sydney he was spotted at the 2005 *Tosca* general rehearsal, although he was whisked away before the scene in which his father joined the insects on the floor. 'We didn't want him to see Cheryl kill me', Coleman-Wright says, smiling. Yet Gabriel understands the difference between reality and play-acting; he made his opera debut in a 2004 Houston Grand Opera production of *Madama Butterfly* in which his mother sang the title role, playing Cio-Cio San's son and later describing the experience as the best of his life.

His parents are ambiguous about the idea of their offspring following in their footsteps. 'The life of a singer is not easy', says Coleman-Wright. 'Besides, we don't want Gabriel to be travelling the world when we're old!' Barker dreams of her son becoming a conductor and offering his parents jobs in their dotage. But if he seriously wanted to be a singer, she would encourage him. 'It's a difficult but fantastic life and if you have the talent and the yearning to do it, it's important to follow that, even if it doesn't work out.'

Home and away

Travelling to Melbourne for the Autumn and Spring seasons, which can last up to eleven weeks each, presents a challenge, especially to singers with children of school age. Some leave their offspring with family or friends in Sydney; others place them in schools in Melbourne.

Emma and Stephen Matthews continue to pay for their son Jack's Sydney childcare to ensure he doesn't lose his place while also hiring a nanny to help out in Melbourne. Lisa Russell flies to Melbourne with baby Chloe while Richard Alexander does the ten-hour drive with the family's two cats and two dogs. In Melbourne the cats stay with Russell's parents while the humans and dogs take up residence in a company-provided serviced apartment in

Left: Bass Richard Alexander, soprano Lisa Russell, daughter Chloe and pets in their Sydney backyard.

St Kilda. Michael Lewis and Nicole Youl's beloved cactus, 'The Boy', given to Youl by Lewis when they first started dating, travels with them wherever they go.

Barker and Coleman-Wright are freelancers, so they do not make the biannual journey to Melbourne. When the time came for Gabriel to go to school they left London and bought a townhouse in Sydney to offer him stability and the proximity of grandparents and cousins. But their lives are still filled with travel.

Gabriel is not averse to it but he has come to expect a certain standard of accommodation. En route to Melbourne recently the family stopped to overnight at a motel, where its youngest member enquired about the whereabouts of the room-service menu. Coleman-Wright had to explain: 'There's no room service here, love—we're in Yass.'

If juggling two demanding careers with the needs of a family is difficult, the sense of camaraderie that comes from working in the same industry more than compensates. 'It's wonderful to go to rehearsals with your best friend', says Barker. Even at home the couple is forever discussing fresh approaches to roles. Yet they can be each other's harshest critics. 'We can be *quite* direct with each other', Coleman-Wright confesses. They don't shy away from expressing their opinions during rehearsals either. 'People who don't know us sometimes think we're having a fall-out!' Barker says, laughing uproariously. They draw the line at practising at home together, however, even though Coleman-Wright is an excellent pianist. 'That's when we have fisticuffs', Barker explains. Her husband insists the aggression is one-sided. 'I'd tell her something is wrong and she'd go, "Okay". And then on the next page I'd make a suggestion and her neck would get a little stiff. And on the next page she'd say: "Let's just forget it!" and storm off.'

Barker admits that as a young singer she sometimes felt envious of her husband's career, which was already established when she joined him in London twenty-odd years ago. In the early days the couple used to remind themselves that they were not competing for the same roles. Now they 'wallow' in each other's success.

Professional jealousy doesn't feature in Richard Alexander and Lisa Russell's marriage either ('Once you have a child you're a team'), and it's certainly not a factor in Michael Lewis and Nicole Youl's relationship. Lewis in fact clucks over his wife, egging her on to spread her wings and try her luck internationally. She has an extraordinary voice, he feels, and she might not be able to realise her potential in Australia, where exposure to a wide range of repertoire is limited.

Youl, however, enjoys the status quo. 'This is the happiest time of my life', she says, referring to her husband's ambitions for her as 'the only little burr in our relationship'. She doesn't want to go back to being a struggling artist.

Right: Back to the score: soprano Emma Matthews at work, rehearsing *Romeo and Juliet*.

Alexander and Russell, who have auditioned successfully in Europe and can legally work there, made a conscious decision to stay in Australia. They love their home life and are convinced Australia is the best place to bring up Chloe. Yet every now and again they wonder what it would be like to try their luck in the big pond...

Emma Matthews never wonders, despite the fact that she has a British passport and a voice that could hold its own on any stage. 'My husband, my children and my home are more important to me', she says. 'Singing is as important as they are, but I don't need international success, or even a career, to be able to sing.'

She did some auditions in Europe a few years ago and describes them as 'a bit of a flop': 'I'm hopeless at being Emma singing an aria.' On stage she becomes the character whose role she's performing.

Matthews' enchantment with home life is illustrated by the fact that she dropped her maiden name, highly unusual for a singer. Perplexed colleagues wanted to know what would happen if they got divorced, but for Matthews it was part of 'the wonderful thing of being married and having the same name as my husband'. She confesses though that if *Lulu* had received bad press she was going to revert to Emma Lysons.

Left: Emma and Stephen Matthews with sons Jack and Brendan at home in Sydney.

Answering the critics

Most singers say they either take reviews with a pinch of salt (an early critic expressed the view that Coleman-Wright would not amount to much), or that they only read the ones that sing their praises. Michael Lewis is the exception—he studies all his notices. He often dislikes them intensely too, and finds the standard of opera criticism in Australia 'abysmal'. Most critics' field of expertise is classical music, he feels, when an opera reviewer should also have knowledge of the voice and the theatre.

Youl is convinced some opera critics have an aversion to the art form and are incapable of writing about it objectively. She has never been disturbed by her own reviews but like her husband, tends to be offended by what is written about him. 'I've contacted a few critics in my time', Lewis smiles.

Emma Matthews doesn't always enjoy her press notices but she learns from them. When at twenty-four she did *Daughter of the Regiment*—too soon, she realises now—one critic felt that she was 'not Dame Joan'.

At the Huntington Festival in NSW a few years later, she sang her first public top F, in an aria from *Mitridate* which she was to perform in Sydney later that year. She remembers being surrounded by barrels of wine, which gave the venue a boomy acoustic. 'This high F came out—it was a bloody good high F and I was very impressed with it—but it had an edge that was unpleasant to some ears.' One reviewer felt it sounded like an electric drill. Matthews was mortified but she took the criticism to heart. Approaching the offending note at the Sydney performance a few months later, she relaxed into it and held it. This time the writer approved.

Opera singers are constantly exposed to criticism, Cheryl Barker points out. The language coach, the repetiteur, the director, the conductor, the press, they all have their say, and any career in opera involves some rejection. 'When you think about it, it's incredible that we can still stand up and do it.'

This is all the more reason why a solid home base where you can let your hair down is crucial. Barker and Coleman-Wright chill out in front of the TV, or on the beach, or at the cinema. They love to take Gabriel swimming, or to play games—Monopoly, Scrabble, cards. Not surprisingly, they tend to socialise with colleagues from the opera world. 'When you've been doing rehearsals with people for six weeks, they become your friends, and after two months they become family', Coleman-Wright says.

Lisa Russell and Richard Alexander relax by doing 'very non-operatic things'—going bush, going to the beach, taking the baby and the dogs to Sydney's Centennial Park or Café Bones in Haberfield (anywhere the dogs are welcome, really). They too, have close friends in the opera community.

When Emma and Stephen Matthews got married, 80% of the guests at their wedding were from the company. Afterwards the minister at Sydney's St Andrew's Cathedral begged the congregation to come back the following Sunday. He said he'd never heard hymns sung like that before.

But since having their own family, home has become an escape from work for the couple. 'Here I am just Emma, not Emma the singer', Matthews says. 'I don't have to try to impress anyone, or be amusing. I can just put on my track suit and be a dag, which is what I am, really.'

When she first joined the mothers' group she attends with Brendan, one of the other women asked her what she did for a living. 'I'm an opera singer', Matthews replied. The other mothers seemed a little taken aback and one asked: 'So who do you sing with?' 'Opera Australia', Matthews said. After a short silence, someone asked: 'Where do they sing?' to which Matthews responded 'At the Opera House'.

'You must be good then', the first mother concluded.

Right: Soprano Nicole Youl, baritone Michael Lewis and their travelling pot plant, 'The Boy', make themselves at home in a Melbourne apartment.

CHAPTER 14

ON THE ROAD

Three hours before the opening of **Oz**Opera's Hobart run of *Carmen* in August 2005, stage crew have all but completed assembling of the set, or the 'bump-in'. As the last of the lights are focused, singers are standing around in jeans and sweaters, waiting to do a sound check.

They rehearsed at the venue the day before, so the musicians are aware they face challenges. For one thing, the Theatre Royal's footlights are the exact height of conductor Patrick Miller's face, so they cannot see him and vice versa. The cast has to follow the conductor's movements through a monitor attached to the upstairs balcony, visible to the stage but not the audience. 'Singers don't look at conductors anyway', someone quips.

A second, more serious obstacle is that the lip of the stage is higher than the pit wall, so that it channels sound from the pit into the auditorium, where it is bounced back to the stage. Singers who responded to this 'echo' at the first rehearsal, discovered that their performance was consistently a fraction of a beat behind the orchestra. They had to learn to sing with the conductor, ahead of the beat, in two hours. 'Touring teaches you new skills', is Patrick Miller's laconic comment.

Learning curve

Professional development is one of the core reasons for **Oz**Opera's existence. Its touring program nurtures emerging singers, conductors, directors and stage crew, who test their mettle in smaller regional theatres before moving on to the mainstage of the Arts Centre and the Opera House.

Touring productions can be a learning experience for audiences too. Assistant director and stage manager Jane Millet, who is walking around the set with an electric drill (she's done five tours with the company) remembers recruiting a jackaroo in Kununurra in

Left: the road to Launceston: driver Bob Dove on his fifth tour with **Oz**Opera.

north-western Australia to help assemble a *La bohème* set. To her surprise, he turned up for the show. Although he lived miles from the nearest town, had never seen an opera and didn't know anything about it, he later told her that he'd loved it.

Above: Tour manager David Harrod pins up pictures of the **Oz**Opera team in Hobart's Theatre Royal.

Right: Mezzo-soprano Tania Ferris listens to feedback during the first sound check in Hobart.

Making do

Compared to some of **Oz**Opera's performance venues, Hobart's beautiful old Theatre Royal, with its embossed decorations and patterned ceilings, is a luxury environment. Anne Frankenberg, who was **Oz**Opera manager until the end of 2005, is used to organising performances in far more primitive venues. In 2004 **Oz**Opera performed *La bohème* in a hay shed in Borden, north of Albany, in Western Australia. Frankenberg, who'd inspected possible performance venues in the region months in advance, remembers that the town had 'about thirty people' in it and no regular space big enough for the set. But it did have a hay shed with a tin roof and sides, filled with hay bales. Frankenberg suggested to the organisers that they block off the open ends with bales and stack more to fashion a foyer and a dressing room. On opening night fire trucks were on standby because it was *La bohème* and Mimi had the candle and the audience was sitting among the bales.

A local farmer's wife had galvanised the community and sold 600 tickets. 'They had people queuing up and begging for seats—they could have sold one hundred more.'

When organising a performance in a regional town, identifying an enthusiastic individual to garner community support is crucial. 'If you can find such a person, the show will be successful whatever the physical resources', Frankenberg says.

The national tour is designed to reach far-flung communities. Spread over three years, in the first year it typically covers Victoria, the Australian Capital Territory (ACT), Tasmania and Queensland, in the second year NSW and South Australia, and the third the Northern Territory and Western Australia. Frankenberg, a clarinettist and MBA graduate, began her career in arts management when she walked into the office of the Victorian State Opera's (VSO) technical director ('I was flogging my CV, as you do') on the day the director needed a new assistant. She says while outback audiences often include people who have never seen opera, in regional centres like Hobart, **Oz**Opera's informal approach is usually cited as the reason for its appeal.

The professional touch

Yet as the cast and orchestra wrap up the sound check and the crew add finishing touches to the set, it's clear that artists' and crew members' dedication to the task at hand is anything but casual. Professionalism rules backstage too. In one of the dressing rooms, wardrobe master Ross Hall is hanging rows of freshly washed and ironed costumes on racks. There are 1950s-style dresses in fuchsia pink and lavender, skirts in shades of yellow and mustard, sexy black tops and steel-grey soldiers' uniforms.

In venues that call for a creative approach, Hall uses costume racks to separate male and female sections of the dressing room. Singers have a relaxed attitude: 'They're professionals. The girls wear dressing gowns so they can get changed under them and the boys walk around in their undies.'

Where necessary Hall lays ensembles out in the wings and gives artists a hand with quick costume changes. He also styles wigs. 'It gets pretty hectic but I don't mind it—you get tired when you sit down.'

Between performances he washes and irons costumes. Most have been dyed so they have to be hand washed in cold water and sometimes the process takes all day. Getting garments dry can be tricky too: in the wet Tasmanian winter, Don Jose's T-shirt, which can't be tumble dried because it will shrink, takes two days to dry. Garments like the soldiers' uniforms, which can only be dry-cleaned, have to go without cleaning for weeks because the company does not stay in one spot long enough. After each performance, Hall also cleans and restyles wigs.

He has toured with the company once before and enjoys the contact with the people and the opportunity to see new places. 'It's like a working holiday', he says. Besides a spell as second-in-charge in the Costume department of the VSO, he has always freelanced, and also has experience as a wardrobe buyer and a dyer. He would like to work full time but wardrobe positions are scarce.

Down the passage from his 'office' is a door that goes through to the stage. On it is a picture of former **Oz**Opera director Richard Gill. Someone has planted a life-sized red kiss on his forehead and written 'The old man is watching you!' underneath his face. On stage, everything is in place for curtain up in just over two hours. Jane Millet, who has put away her electric drill, checks props that have been arranged on a table.

The set is dominated by a huge steel wall which opens and closes at various points of the production. By contrast, the back wall is painted orange, which complements the colours of the women's costumes.

Director Adam Cook and designer Stephen Curtis, who also gave **Oz**Opera its popular *La bohème* production, set *Carmen* in the mid-20th century because Spanish costumes from the original period would have blown the budget, and because 1950s' attire made women look sexy. This suits an opera that, in Cook's words, 'explores what happens when the organ that does your thinking is not your brain'.

To Stephen Curtis the piece was also about the tension between opposites, the personalities of the main characters personifying extremes. His set, with its back wall painted in 'passionate' orange, incorporates the shades of the sunset associated with the women, while the cold steel of the second wall links it visually to the soldiers' uniforms.

The steel wall functions as a symbol of both freedom and enclosure. When Carmen and Don José ride off to the mountains at the end of Act II, it opens up, enabling them to run off. Yet at the end of the opera, when he says to her, 'Don't you love me?', the wall closes behind them, as if to confirm that she's not going anywhere.

Size matters

Like Carmen, the director of a touring production faces many challenges. For one thing, the entire show has to be able to fit into a truck (Cook refers to the regional tour as 'the opera caravan') and the set has to be designed so that it can be installed in the afternoon and performed the next night.

Left: Tania Ferris applies her makeup in the Ladies, Theatre Royal.

Above: Wardrobe crates backstage at the Theatre Royal.

Right: Tenor Bradley Daley gives Tania Ferris a helping hand with her costume.

Working with a reduced score (which implies a shrunken chorus) requires further adjustments. In Sydney, Cook remembered going through the reworked score with Gill. The conductor had kept the famous tunes, which audiences expected to hear, but he'd axed the expensive chorus scenes in which they occurred. Thus, the music of the bullfighters' parade was included without the bullfighters, and the cigarette girls had been reduced from forty to four. The way to embrace such a reduction, Cook felt, was to reinvent it as though it was what the piece had always been.

Time constraints presented obstacles of their own: with only three weeks' rehearsal time, Cook could allow no time for experimentation. 'I had to walk in and say: "Here's the design presentation and now we're going to start."' In such circumstances singers depended on the director for guidance, which Cook sometimes found 'dispiriting'. One singer asked him when he wanted her to come in. 'Just before you sing would be good', he replied. He found Gill great to work with and 'like all conductors', decidedly opinionated. 'Every conductor will tell you that no company ever performs the piece as it's written and that this one will be the first to do so.'

As a final complication, **Oz**Opera's directors have to rehearse a double cast, since if a soloist comes down with flu in Kununurra, the nearest replacement might be six hours away. Soloists alternate nights on centre stage with nights in the chorus, and if a principal does not appear in every act (the toreador, for example) he would be expected to perform a chorus part in other acts. A very versatile member of the company once played five different roles in a week, and on one memorable occasion one of the Don Josés grabbed the wrong girl. 'I'm *not* Carmen tonight!' she hissed at him.

Cook, who is artistic director of the State Theatre Company of South Australia, directed **Oz**Opera's production of Jonathan Mills and Dorothy Porter's *The Ghost Wife,* which led to the *La bohème* touring production. In 2006 he directed OA's *Lakmé*.

On the stage and in the pit, the sound check has been wrapped up. Some cast and crew members are waiting at the bus outside the theatre; others have started walking the five-odd blocks back to the hotel. There, cast members disappear upstairs to get ready for the evening's show.

Even when there's no performance, those who prefer to keep to themselves are free to do so. Tour manager David Harrod, who is going through paperwork with stage manager Jane Millet in the hotel lobby, says that in his Day One speech to the company he always stresses that members need to give each other space.

Running the show

Jane Millet says while some people are tour animals who 'rock up in a new place and are out the next morning, having a great time' others find it stressful to be away from loved ones and a familiar environment, and disruptive to pull up roots every second day.

Travelling by bus gets very tiring and people get cranky, she says. Although 'hissy fits' are allowed, delivering them to fellow cast members is *verboten*. 'David and I welcome people coming to us with issues and if it's something that needs resolving we'll do it. In a situation like this, stewing on something can be destructive.'

Millet focuses on organising the truck, set and crew while Harrod, who also managed the 2004 tour, looks after personnel issues and travel logistics, including contact with sponsors, ticketing, promotion and overseeing contracts with local presenters. It's a job that requires constant explanation and cajoling.

One presenter, for example, didn't realise he was responsible for selling tickets rather than **Oz**Opera. Another forgot to budget for casuals—he was going to ask backpackers in a touristy Outback town to help assemble the set, yet the idea of voluntary work didn't appeal to the travellers. The company was staying in a hotel that was flanked by a caravan park. Harrod remembers walking around it with a torch light, Millet by his side, looking for helpers to build the set.

Millet recalls the time the company was going to perform on a basketball court and organisers planned to place the orchestra behind the stage. 'We had to have a chat; go through some details', she says.

But whatever hiccups may occur, the show always goes on. 'If the truck didn't turn up, the performance would go on in concert version', Harrod says. 'When you have an audience waiting there are no excuses.'

He worked as a casual staging assistant for the Melbourne Symphony Orchestra before joining Orchestra Victoria as assistant manager, then returning to the MSO as production manager. Now a freelancer, in 2005 he spent six months managing the **Oz**Opera regional tour.

Millet, who in the same year toured with **Oz**Opera for the fifth time (she's been around Australia twice with the company), is also a freelancer. A theatre graduate, the longest she spent in full-time employment was two years as senior stage manager for Melbourne Theatre Company. In 2005 she worked as stage manager for **Oz**Opera and MTC and as production coordinator for the Melbourne Festival. In 2006 she directed *Carmen*, as Adam Cook was not available.

For her, the **Oz**Opera attraction lies partly in the opportunity to become part of local communities through recruiting and working with crew members. 'They'd rock up and the

Left: Tenor Mattias Lower adjusts his cap before taking to the stage as a soldier.

doors of the truck would open and they'd almost faint at the size of the stuff; they'd be unable to understand how it's going to happen', she laughs.

Millet also loves helping to bring opera to people who may not otherwise have an opportunity to see it. 'When you're doing a semi-staged performance in Jamberoo in the Northern Territory, and you have to call the audience for 7.30 p.m. in order to start at 8 p.m., and the interval runs for half an hour because they're having gherkins and cheese cubes on sticks and everyone's in shorts and thongs and it's the first opera they've ever heard, it's just magic.'

She has particularly fond memories of the 650-strong audience who were 'gas-bagging' in a shed in an Outback town (it shall remain unnamed), making such a racket that the orchestra could not tune. 'They'd rolled off the buses pissed to begin with, and then just continued', Millet says. She took a microphone, went on stage and announced: 'Ladies and gentlemen, could you please take your seats so the orchestra can tune!' at which someone at the back shouted: 'Show us your tits!' The performance was a resounding success.

Above: Horn player Jules Evans warms up before entering the pit at the Theatre Royal.

Right: Conductor Patrick Miller awaits his call on opening night in Hobart.

If Millet enjoys regional audiences, as assistant director she finds constantly changing venues a challenge. In a fixed venue, once entrances and positions have been established singers can concentrate on their performance, but on the road every venue is different. As for stage management: labelling is the key. 'Every nut, bolt and prop has a sticker on it—if we all had an accident, someone else could put the show together.' Millet deposits props on a table in the wings, from where the cast picks them up. She doesn't cue singers. 'I don't expect artists to stand around like warm props, waiting to be pushed on stage—I'm all for responsibility.' She does call lights to the head electrician.

As she leaves to grab a bite before the show, singer Tiffany Speight, David Harrod's wife, arrives from Sydney to join him for the weekend. Other artists' partners arrived from Sydney and Melbourne earlier in the day. Tenor Bradley Daley's eldest child was born on an **Oz**Opera tour and although his family has since expanded, his wife still visits him on some weekends.

Some artists don't see their families while on tour. Baritone Francesco Fabris, who has done many tours with the company, has a wife and two young boys in Melbourne. He says his sons have grown up knowing that he sometimes goes away but he always comes back.

Fortunately for those far away from home, the tour offers some opportunities for

domesticity: in the green room at the Theatre Royal, Jane Millet has put up a cleaning roster for company members. There are also mugs, coffee, tea bags and milk and sugar for cast members.

A chorus member who covers for the role of Micaela is trying to style her hair in a pony tail with fringe in front of a mirror. 'Do you think I look like a virgin?' she asks photographer Bridget Elliot. 'No', says Elliot. 'Okay', says the soprano, adjusting her hairstyle. 'I didn't think so.' A group of singers meander past on their way to their dressing room, chattering and giggling, some singing at top volume.

Left: Mezzo-soprano Karma Nordqvist signs posters in the green room.

Music in the moment

On a dilapidated black leather coach underneath the TV screen on which the show is to be projected, the clarinettist is operating on his reed with a cigarette filter. A colleague from the wind section is telling a tale about working with a conductor who had a predilection for slow tempos. 'In the end we had to tell him: "Move it! We're running out of breath!"' The clarinettist rolls his eyes. A crew member arrives, enquiring after the whereabouts of a missing extension chord. 'It's in the orchestra's dressing room', an orchestra member tells him. 'We had to switch off the heater in the pit because it was humming at an awkward pitch—it was too distracting.'

'Apparently the area underneath the stage used to be a brothel', announces conductor Patrick Miller, who has sunk into the black leather coach with a mug of steaming tea. 'And it's supposed to have a ghost.'

Not that the thought is making him nervous. 'There's no time to get panicky around here', he says. Originally a double bassist, Miller did a music degree at the Victorian College of the Arts and started conducting when he and friends staged Act I from *The Marriage of Figaro* in their final year. He was halfway through a Masters in Conducting when Richard Gill offered him the *Carmen* tour. He intends returning to Uni to finish his Masters.

At 25, Miller's biggest challenge has been to gain the respect of older, more experienced orchestral musicians and cast members (only one orchestral player is younger than him). He built credibility by being 'very polite' and by thinking carefully before asking 'someone in their 40s' to sing or play a phrase in a particular way. 'The big maestro act definitely wouldn't have worked here', he says, taking a mouthful of tea.

Although he finds opera conducting 'absolutely thrilling' and feels completely at home in the theatre, it took a while to get his head around the reduction. The orchestra consists of eleven instrumentalists—five winds, five strings and a keyboard that doubles as percussionist—and to get used to the sound they make, Miller stopped listening to recordings of the opera months before rehearsals started. Now he's 'staggered' by the volume the tiny ensemble manages to produce.

Weeks before in Sydney, **Oz**Opera artistic director Richard Gill (he has since left the company) confessed that he was frequently intimidated by the prospect of having to reduce

opera scores written for sixty orchestral players for an ensemble of eleven. 'You're playing with big people's toys', he said. Yet having arranged *The Magic Flute*, *The Barber of Seville*, *Rigoletto*, *La bohème* and *Carmen* in this way, he also loved the insight into composers' minds that the process afforded him.

Before deciding who would play what in the reduction, Gill would study every note in the score, unravelling the way in which the composer had conceived the melody and harmonic progression. In *Carmen*, as in most operas, the strings play the body of the music, and in the reduction Gill would leave their parts largely unchanged. The reduced wind section, however, would have to represent everything from piccolo to bass trombone. 'It's like putting together a mosaic; the pieces are all there but you have to represent them faithfully.' If he ran into difficulty he would check the score to see what the composer had done. Occasionally, he would make the thrilling discovery that he and Bizet had found the same solution to a problem. Yet sometimes Bizet would have done something completely different. 'That's when you say to yourself: "Okay, he's a genius and I'm not."'

Singers wander in and out of the green room throughout the performance, following the show on the TV monitor, chatting and having tea. During interval a chocolate cake is produced to celebrate someone's

Tonight's Carmen, mezzo-soprano Judith Dodsworth, adjusts her wig.

birthday, the number of candles on it causing a lengthy dispute. After the show company members leave through Stage Door, where the bus is waiting.

On Friday night the performance has been all but sold out and in the foyer of the Theatre Royal the audience is buzzing. Some are having wine with friends; others are studying the photographs of the cast that David Harrod has put up in the foyer. Inside the auditorium they keep chatting to acquaintances as far as three rows away, but an expectant hush falls when Miller ascends the podium and takes a bow. When the orchestra starts playing, it fills the auditorium with a surprising volume of sound.

The cast sing in English, their clear diction allowing patrons to follow most of the dialogue. Surtitles would present impossible technical obstacles in many of the venues where the company performs and **Oz**Opera surveys show that regional audiences overwhelmingly prefer text sung in English.

In the hotel foyer the next morning Harrod finds a review in a local newspaper. The critic, although complimentary about some aspects of the **Oz**Opera production, complains that in his opinion principals didn't always look the part, and laments the fact that Hobart is unable to see OA's full-blown productions. Harrod shrugs. He puts the paper away when he sees singers approaching.

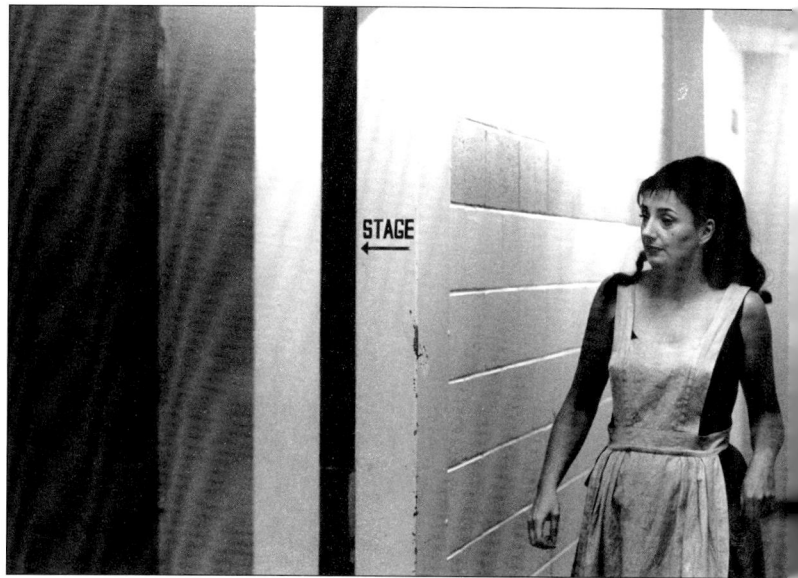

Judith Dodsworth makes her way to the stage.

On Saturday night the company gives its final performance in Hobart. Backstage in the green room, orchestra members reveal that the off-pitch heater has been reinstated out of earshot, from where it now 'toasts' half the pit while leaving the other half semi-frozen. Temperature variations are causing pitch variations, since in the strings section of the pit the heat is making instruments go flat. 'You make adjustments', is the philosophical response of concertmaster Iseult Stephenson.

Most orchestral musicians agree that for them, an **Oz**Opera tour is a sought-after 'gig'. When playing for opera or ballet, pit musicians have little interaction with the stage, yet on tour it is not unusual for them to sit in front of the stage, or even on it, so that players have a sense of being part of the show. Travelling on the bus with cast and crew, they become part of the performing company on a social level too.

Stephenson, a violinist with Orchestra Victoria, says getting to know her colleagues in the **Oz**Opera band has increased the joy of performing with them. 'In a big orchestra you can spend years saying hello to people with whom you never actually have a conversation.'

As concertmaster she oversees bowings and makes sure that the strings blend, a tall order in such a small group. This is her sixth **Oz**Opera tour and she says it took time to adjust to being one of two violinists when in Orchestra Victoria she's one of twenty-five. She has learned to treat the reduction as chamber music. 'We really have to listen to each other to get the balance between the wind and the string sections right.'

Although there are five each of wind and string instruments, because the winds carry more they have to play more softly (sometimes a carpet is placed under the section to muffle their sound) while strings have to play as loudly as they can.

In the hotel lobby late the next morning, a few bleary-eyed singers have gathered. They are waiting for companions who have not yet risen to join them on a Sunday outing. Apparently there was a party in someone's room the previous night…

'It is a festive atmosphere and living in hotels, things occasionally get a little raucous', smiles David Harrod, who has come downstairs in search of coffee for his laryngitis-stricken wife.

In the driver's seat

Also in the foyer, bus driver Bob Dove is waiting for cast members who have signed up to join him on an excursion to the historic town of Richmond, a forty-five-minute drive from Hobart. A professional tour operator, Dove has driven **Oz**Opera around Australia since 1997. 'One day', he remembers, 'my boss said to me, "Dovey, I've got a nice job for you—you can go away with the opera people". I said: "What the hell do I know about opera?"'

For its inaugural *Barber of Seville* tour, Dove drove the company around South Australia, Victoria and NSW 'and it was fabulous'. He loved seeing how a production came together, something of which until then he'd had no idea. 'You'd arrive at a venue and have a look around and say to the crew: "You're going to stage an opera *here?*"' To see basketball courts and aircraft hangars transformed into opera houses, and 'ordinary folk' into performers, was fascinating.

Hiccups there have been, like the time in Geelong when the coach, which had been parked uphill, wouldn't start after the show and the cast had to help to push-start it. But Dove comes back every year because he gets to know the singers and loves watching them improve with each performance. He has come to enjoy comparing the merits of various performances too, and these days he even buys the occasional ticket to an opera performance at Melbourne's Arts Centre.

On Monday morning he is waiting outside the coach, where by 8 a.m. most company members have deposited their luggage and instruments. No sooner has the bus left Hobart for Launceston, where **Oz**Opera is to perform on Tuesday night, than Jane Millet starts

Left: Patrick Miller and repetiteur David McSkimming await the tour bus' departure for Launceston.

Above: Stage manager and assistant director Jane Millett entertains baritone Francesco Fabris and soprano Jocelyn Hickey.

organising passengers into teams for the Tasmanian leg of the Ozzie Opera Trivia Contest. Competition for the prize—a key ring with a Tasmanian devil on it, valued at $1—is fierce, and teams who resort to the use of mobile phones (at one point all four members of a particular side are seen conferring with Sydney and Melbourne associates) elicit loud reprisals from players whose phones have no reception in the area.

Touring's attractions

Without ambition no performer will get very far, and many of the singers who work for **Oz**Opera aim for the mainstage, where some have already performed. Yet the company also employs established singers. Tenor Bradley Daley (one of the Don Josés) is on his third **Oz**Opera tour (he was Rodolfo in its earlier *La bohème* production) and is based in London, from where he freelances, mostly for English National Opera. For Daley and his family, a regional tour provides an opportunity to see loved ones in Melbourne, where he used to work for the VSO.

Above: Annarosa Berman interviews Bradley Daley en route from Hobart to Launceston.

Right: Patrick Miller and David McSkimming accompany singers at a high-school performance in Launceston.

Daley enjoys the regional tour for its own sake too: the first opera he saw changed his life and he loves being in a position to offer others the same experience. But although he derives pleasure from the sense of camaraderie that develops among company members on tour, he says being part of a group can sometimes be lonely too.

Mezzo-soprano Tania Ferris, one of the Carmens, is on her first tour with **Oz**Opera, having graduated from **Oz**Opera's Schools Company. The regional tour is a cruise by comparison, she says. 'Singers who work for Schools Company drive the van from venue to venue, set up the show without help from crew, put on their costumes and makeup, do their vocal warm-ups, perform, talk to the children, pack it all up and drive on to the next school. They do this 200 times a year.'

Ferris, who completed her BMus Ed in Perth, taught for six years before enrolling for a Masters in Performance, which led to the Schools Company job. She went to New York for four months to learn the role of Carmen with singer/teacher Joshua Hecht. Since she's single, being away from home is easy. 'The most difficult part of touring is having too many opportunities for shopping!' After the tour she plans to audition for roles in New York and London.

Frank (his full name is Francesco) Fabris, one of the Escamillos, is married with two young boys and on his fourth tour with **Oz**Opera. Before that he did six years of freelancing

for Schools Company and the VSO, and he's done minor roles for OA. A qualified nurse ('it's one of the few jobs that enables you to drop everything to go on tour'), in Melbourne he works shifts at a hospital. He has not had a full-time job in twenty years and enjoys touring with **Oz**Opera because he loves singing and because it enables him to get away from the pressures of his other job.

In Launceston, where the touring party arrives in the early afternoon, it's raining cats and dogs. Singers and instrumentalists scheduled to perform a short program at a local school check into the hotel first. 'I'm having a bad makeup day', soprano Jocelyn Hickey later announces, as Bob Dove pulls away from a set of traffic lights. She is dressed in Micaela's powder blue 1950s' costume and attempting to balance lipstick on a hand mirror while applying mascara with her other hand. 'I'll be here to pick you up, Darling', Dove assures her as she gets off. 'In an outfit like that you're likely to receive an offer you may not be able to refuse.'

The session is attended by fifteen high school students, mostly girls. They are baffled by the volume of the sound emanating from the singers' chests and ask questions about the manner of its production.

Back at the hotel, crew members unload the set in pouring rain, and by 8 a.m. on Tuesday morning the bump-in at the Princess Theatre across the road is in full swing. The head mechanist has explained the procedure to local crew, a mixture of theatre staff and volunteers. Millet is once again walking around with her electric drill. By midday the lights are being focused.

By 7 p.m., Millet is making the first of the evening's series of backstage announcements to the cast and crew: 'Ladies and Gentlemen of the *Carmen* company, this is your half-hour call. The theatre is open and the stage is live!'

In the foyer of the Princess Theatre, Launceston's opera lovers have started arriving for the evening's performance, disposing of their umbrellas and raincoats and chatting excitedly while queuing for wine and rearranging their wet hair. Exhilaration is in the air.

It's a scene that brings to mind Richard Gill's view of opera as having the potential to deliver something 'extraordinary' to audiences. 'People look for something beyond the mundane, and opera, with its heightened sense of reality, provides it—that's why it's so important.'

Ensuring the survival of the art form means searching far and wide for new audiences to captivate and enthrall, through repertoire that speaks straight to the heart. As OA chief executive Adrian Collette puts it: 'The fundamental thing we do to create new audiences is we produce *La bohème*, *Tosca, Carmen*, because that is where people's operatic journeys begin.'

He is optimistic that OA is succeeding in the quest to bring 'something extraordinary' to an ever-expanding public. 'I sense that the cultural virtues of companies like OA are being better understood in the broader community.'

Left: Orchestra Victoria cellist Sarah Cuming. Her instrument accompanies her as a paid-up passenger from Launceston to Melbourne.

CHAPTER 15

THE COMPANY WE KEEP

Opera companies do not just appear. They grow out of communities.

'They are the peek representation of every student playing an instrument, or acting in a play, or painting a picture', says OA chief executive, Adrian Collette. You don't have to be Renée Fleming to appreciate first-class singing, but if you've sung in a choir you are better equipped to understand what an opera company does.

OA's artistic leadership, though optimistic about the company's future, is realistic about the challenges that face those who set out to produce opera in Australia.

In the next half-century of its existence, says Collette, the company will have to expand its involvement in music education. But while he hopes this leads to a broader support base, he passionately believes that audiences are primarily built through investment in the great works of the repertoire, which speak to humanity as directly as Michelangelo's paintings. 'These operas are amongst Western Civilisation's finest creations and nothing will guarantee our future audience more than performing them.'

Collette also believes that OA has a duty to nurture Australian artistry—the Neil Armfields, Barrie Koskys, Baz Luhrmanns and Lisa Gasteens of the future. And he hopes that by the time the company celebrates its sixtieth birthday, the Capital Fund, $9 million strong in 2006, will have swelled to $50 million. 'We are not building reserves to get rich; we are strengthening the company to enable us to invest in interesting new Australian and international repertoire.'

Board chairman Gordon Fell says although it is generally appreciated that opera contributes to 'the creation of an interesting, multi-faceted society', in a world where the

Left: Cameron Anderson awaits his cue to go on stage in *Tosca*.

logic of economics would demand an end to funding for arts organisations, there are no guarantees. To him, the challenge of the next fifty years will be to ensure the company's survival. Fell balances this 'slightly negative though legitimate' aim with a more upbeat one: to perform in the emerging houses of Asia as part of Australia's integration into the region. 'We will have to be very patient and keep strengthening the company financially, but in twenty or thirty years we may be able to do it.'

OA's executive producer Stuart Maunder is 'very optimistic' about the company's future ('We do amazing things with limited resources') but he dreams of better subsidised (i.e. cheaper) tickets and a respite for some of the most popular pieces in the repertoire. What the company demands of *The Magic Flute* is unfair, he feels. 'Next to God it's one of my favourite things, but you'd like people to be able to rediscover it, rather than to think, Do I really have to see it again?'

Music director Richard Hickox looks forward to the Opera House renovations, which should deliver a bigger pit with a better acoustic. 'We are building and building the ensemble with singers of greater and greater ability, and the chorus and orchestra have improved immeasurably since the late 1990s', he says. 'But until we get a decent acoustic, there is a limit to how far we can go.' Hickox dreams of an outcome that fuses the beauty of the Opera House with the State Theatre's terrific acoustic. 'There would be nothing like it.'

He also envisages an international recording profile for OA (it recorded *The Love for Three Oranges* on the Chandos label in 2005), as a means of 'getting the word around about the great work it is doing'.

Much of that 'great work' is done at the Opera Centre and backstage at the Opera House and the Arts Centre, where in fifty years, the national company and its previous incarnations have survived and thrived thanks to the skill and devotion of its staff. With a few notable exceptions, the company has found ways to accommodate the strong-minded, creative people who are its life blood, while they in turn have thrived on the opportunities it offers. Indeed a measure of the company's appeal is that staff members who wish to transfer to different departments sometimes wait for years for positions to become available.

Design manager Linda Matthews is one staff member who, to her own astonishment, succeeded in moving sideways within the company. In the mid-1980s she was head of the Art department, which at the time involved exposure to dangerous sprays and dyes. As union delegate she called a strike which went to Arbitration Court and led to the installation of fans in the company's George Street headquarters. A few years later she again found herself in Arbitration Court, this time arguing for more natural light for seamstresses at the

Opera Centre in Elizabeth Street. As the management representative of the time stormed past her, Matthews thought: 'Oh well, there goes my career.'

But the opposite happened: she has been with the opera company for over two decades now and thanks partly to the fuss she created, OA became a spearhead for occupational health and safety reforms in the theatre industry. 'Management looked beyond the personal and recognised that I was trying to achieve something that would ultimately benefit us all', she recalls. 'It was fantastic.'

OA's story has been fantastic in many ways. Today it is one of the busiest opera companies in the world, and in a typical year it gives around 230 performances in two cities, attended by well over 300,000 people. **Oz**Opera performs to an additional 97,000 patrons a year, and about 70,000 attendees enjoy the annual Opera in the Domain.

Adrian Collette does not exaggerate when he says: 'It is amazing that an opera company of this scale and standing has been developed in Australia. Given the financial hurdles we've faced, it's a miracle we're here at all.'

The show goes on: soprano Lisa Harper-Brown is made up for *Dido and Aeneas*.

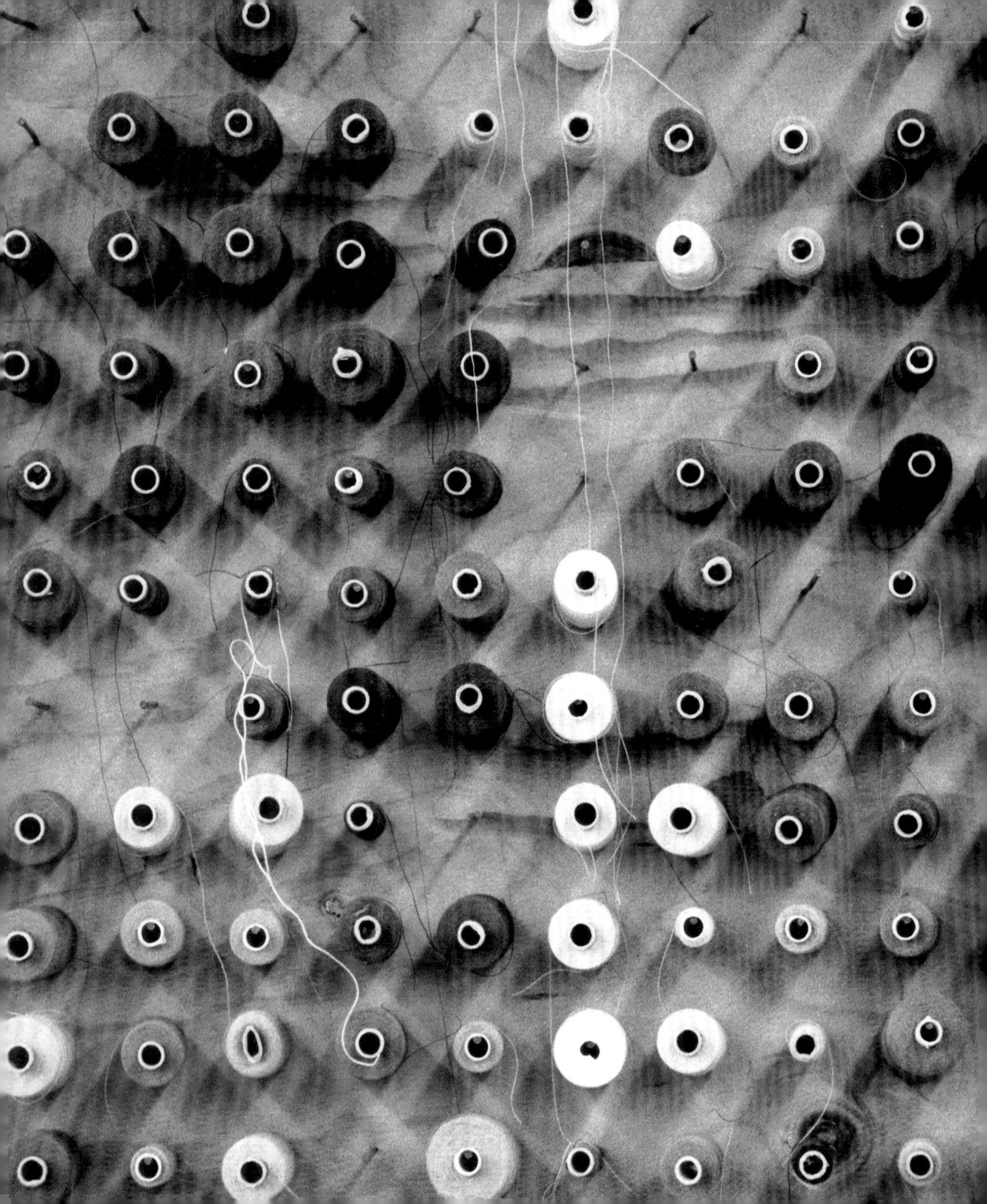

INDEX

Left: Cotten reels in Wardrobe.